The Autism Mom's Survival Guide

Stephanie Hemenway

The Autism Mom's Survival Guide

Copyright ©2009 Stephanie Hemenway

ISBN-10: 1-4392-2661-X
ISBN-13: 9781439226612

Library of Congress Control Number: 2009900887

Printed in the United States of America.

Contents

Introduction

I am a mom. Not just any mom, though. I am the mother of a wonderful, loving, funny, intuitive, completely non-verbal 4-year-old boy who was diagnosed with Autism Spectrum Disorder, which also makes me an Autism Mom. I am far from alone; every twenty minutes, a new mom joins our ranks. *Once every twenty minutes.*

Since you are reading this book, I'll bet that you, too, will never forget the day your child got "the diagnosis." A nice doctor, often a pediatric neurologist, calmly informs us that our child is suffering from Autism Spectrum Disorder, a lifelong psychiatric disorder of which little is known, and suggests that we may wish to look into speech, occupational, and/or physical therapy, which may not be covered by insurance. We are handed our little report and basically told to have a nice day. I know a mother who was actually told "Good luck." Good *luck?*

I remember looking at my son (who was at that moment in total meltdown on the floor of the pediatric neurologist's office) and thinking to myself, *"So what do we do now?"* There was no handbook, no emergency hotline I could call that would tell me how to help my child recover or even *cope* with this disorder. Like every other family, we had to wing it, researching treatments on our own, and learning mostly by trial and error. For a long time daily life was chaotic. I was exhausted, slowly figuring out systems for keeping track of everything we were doing, attempting to help my son, and trying to remember to shower regularly.

As I met other moms of kids with ASD, one thing became very clear—we were *all* reinventing the wheel. Most of the techniques we use at home to keep things running smoothly were discovered by trial and error, and were often nearly identical to what other moms had also discovered on their own.

And these techniques *work!* Over the last couple years I've been privileged to see many incredible Autism Moms in action. Each one has come up with great ideas that could work for anyone. Annette, for example, has a flawless system for setting up a week's worth of supplements at once, is a biomedical encyclopedia and can get her kids to eat *anything.* Susan, a mother I met at speech therapy, has a perfectly orchestrated "sibling drop-off-and-pick-up" system worked out with her mother so that her older son doesn't have to wait through two hours of therapy. (She also manages to be immaculately groomed, with perfect hair and makeup, at all times, which you just can't help but admire.)

As moms in the trenches, we all joke about "not getting the Autism Instruction Manual." And after talking to shell-shocked moms of newly diagnosed kids, and remembering how hard those first months were for me, I decided to put what's worked for me, and for other moms I know, into a simple "survival guide." I thought it needed to be short, to the point, and easy-to-use as a reference because Heaven knows we don't have much free time.

It is my hope that you'll take what you can use from this guide, modify the suggestions to best fit your family, and simply jettison what you don't feel applies. No single system is going to work for every family or for every kid. But on the other hand, there's not much sense in each of us having to totally reinvent the wheel, either. Best wishes to you all as you undertake this amazing journey.

Acknowledgments

I'd like to thank Catherine Harbor, MD, who started my son on his beautiful path to recovery; Annette Van Dyke, the best mentor anyone could be blessed with; Mary Megson, MD; Kyle Van Dyke, MD; and Dan Rossignol, MD, for their commitment to unraveling the puzzle that is ASD; my husband John, for his unflagging love and support; my son, Andrew, whose courage and joy humble us all; and the moms in the trenches from whom I have learned so much.

CHAPTER ONE

On the Home Front

Taking Care of Yourself First

We have all listened to flight attendants remind us that in the unlikely event of a loss of cabin pressure, *we should put on our own masks* before assisting the person next us. This is really pretty sound advice.

I don't know about you, but when we first got the dreaded "autism diagnosis," I sure felt like all the air got sucked out of that room. And what did I do? I tossed my mask aside and put all my energy into helping my son.

After six months of battling autism I was totally exhausted and burned out. And most of the other moms I met were in the same condition.

So I came up with a program for the Basic Care and Feeding of the Autism Mom—me. There is a good reason why this is the *first* section rather than the *last* one—it's an important first step to survival. I realized that I couldn't keep running at the pace I'd set for myself and expect to finish this marathon, and neither can you. It's not selfish to take care of yourself first, it's *critical.*

Boost your nutrition

Raising a child with ASD is a lot like training for a Triathlon—it requires extra nutritional support to maintain the necessary stamina. Unless you are one of the three women in America who actually eats a balanced diet including 5–7 servings of fruits and vegetables every day, you probably need a daily multivitamin, a high-potency B-complex, a calcium supplement, and 1000 mg of extra Vitamin C. Adding a zinc supplement and a cod liver oil capsule daily will provide immune support, and keep you from catching every bug that comes along. It's amazing how many moms (and dads) extol the benefits of good diet and nutritional supplements for their kids, and ignore their own nutritional needs. Pick up a weekly pill-sorter container at the drugstore so you don't forget. Once you start, you'll notice a difference in your energy level within a week.

Get the sleep you need

A lot of Autism Moms suffer from too little sleep, and are chronically fatigued as a result. Everyone needs at least 7–8 hours to function well. If you're not getting that much, *assign yourself a bedtime*, and try turning off the TV or computer an hour before that time. Listen to music or read instead, both of which encourage sleep. If you still are having problems falling or staying asleep, melatonin and 5-HTP (both available at the health-food store) are safer, more natural alternatives to over-the-counter or prescription sleep aids.

Put yourself together in the morning

It's really not a *rule* that stay-at-home moms have to wear sweats 24/7, and stealing ten minutes in the morning to brush your hair and do a quick "mascara and lip gloss" can improve your whole day.

Work out every day... really!

Spending an hour at the gym is just a dim memory for most Autism Moms, but five minutes of stretching followed by another five minutes with a couple of light free weights (dumbbells) can keep you in better shape than you think. Do it first thing in the morning and you'll have more energy all day.

Find that ever-elusive balance between work and home

Good scheduling can make a huge difference to us and our families. Take the initiative and coordinate with your employer to establish a *realistic* work schedule that you can both live with. Working something out in advance is far better than having to address it later at an unfavorable annual review. Most moms discover that if you get pulled in too many different directions, you'll rapidly end up stressed out and too exhausted to be effective at work or at home.

Stay connected with adults

Being a stay-at-home mom can be isolating, and even more so when you have a child on the autism spectrum. Try to talk to at least one person who is old enough to vote (and isn't married to you) during the day.

Keep up with world events

No Autism Mom has the free time to read a daily paper, much less watch in-depth TV news analysis, but that's no reason to be totally unaware of what's going on in the world. Subscribe to a weekly news magazine like *The Week* (my personal favorite), *Time*, or *Newsweek*. You can read it cover-to-cover in less than an hour, and it will allow you to have to have grown-up conversations with adults about something besides poop.

Get an MP3 player

This was Jenny McCarthy's suggestion and it bears repeating. It's a great way to tune out the chaos on "one of those days" and you don't have to be a computer wiz to use it. (Even I managed to figure it out in my own technologically-challenged way.)

Schedule in a half-hour hour "break" every day

Plunk your kids in front of a video for half an hour. Find a "mom only" room and have a cup of tea, listen to quiet music, call a friend, or do absolutely nothing. Don't use it to check your email.

Get away for 3 hours every week

Even the best moms need a break now and then. Pick your day and time, find a sitter, or negotiate with your husband—in short, do whatever you need to do in order to disappear for at least 3 hours once a week. Get a massage, wander through Barnes and Noble, play golf, go fishing, see a movie, do whatever it is you need to do to recharge and regroup. *Warning: Do not fall into the trap of using your time to run errands.* There is nothing relaxing in that.

Schedule couch time

After your kids go to bed, tidy up, fill out the daily report (see page 26), and curl up with your spouse and/or the family pets and watch a movie.

Laugh

Hard. Out loud. At least once a day. Laughter releases endorphins, which boost the immune system.

At the end of the day...

Think of one thing you did just for *yourself* that is entirely unrelated to autism. If you can't think of one, you're not taking care of yourself.

Minimizing Sensory Overload

Preventing sensory overload can do more than anything else to make life at home easier for you, your child, and your whole family.

Many of our kids suffer from what experts call "sensory integration disorder" as well as leaky gut and a slew of other biomedical difficulties. To get a feel for this, imagine having a really bad case of the flu, or the measles. (The latter actually happened to me when I was twenty-five, in spite of having been vaccinated as a child.) Talk about sensory overload... your head hurts, your stomach hurts, light hurts your eyes, noise hurt your ears, your body aches, food smells and tastes awful, and your skin actually hurts all over. (If somebody dragged you to the supermarket when you felt like that, you'd probably cover your ears and scream, too!) My bout with the measles lasted less than a week. Some of our little guys have been dealing with this every day for *years*, and it accounts for a *lot* of their meltdowns.

Although a lot of people use the terms interchangeably, meltdowns are different than *temper tantrums*, which are addressed later on. Meltdowns, which are caused by sensory overload rather than frustration, are more like panic attacks than anything else, and usually start with the child clapping his hands over his ears, rapidly progressing to screaming, spinning, sometimes head-banging, and finally melting into a puddle on the floor.

So to make his life easier, I went through my house and tried to see, hear, smell, touch, and taste the way my son does. These are some of the changes we made that helped to virtually eliminate meltdowns caused by simple sensory overload at our house.

Staging your house

Staging is a term used by realtors to describe furnishing a house so that it has just enough in it to look occupied rather than empty, with no clutter. (I discovered this when we put our house up for sale a few years ago, and our realtor suggested putting half of what we owned into temporary storage.)

Staging your own house, or at least critical parts of it, is probably the single most important thing you can do to help your child function better at home.

Did you ever wonder why so many kids can focus better in therapy than they can at home? It could be in large part because rooms used for therapy are designed with as little distraction as possible. Next time you take your kid to speech, OT, or ABA, look around. Notice how little clutter is in evidence. Now take a hard look at your family room when you get home. By comparison, it's like expecting our kids to live in the toy section of Walmart. It's no wonder so many of them are in a constant state of sensory overload!

You do not need to hire a professional organizer to stage your house—you can actually accomplish it in a single day if you can find a sitter or grandparent to watch your kids at their house. (Getting your kids and husband out of the way is *imperative* to the success of this operation.) If the whole idea seems overwhelming, you can follow the directions below step-by-step, or you can just use it as a general guideline, as long as you end up with the same results.

You'll need the following items:

◆ Black industrial strength trash bags
◆ Gallon zipper bags
◆ 4 large cardboard boxes that can be closed tightly (2' x 2' is a manageable size)
◆ 3-shelf bookcase, no more than 30 inches tall (if finances are tight, check your local thrift stores, or make one out of blocks and boards)
◆ 6 small wicker baskets (available from Bed, Bath & Beyond or Dollar Tree, depending on your budget)
◆ Small plastic milk crate (approximately 10" x 10" with holes in the bottom)
◆ Larger wicker basket (one that would fit 2 large rolls of paper towels)
◆ Colored marking tape (4-color pack, also from Dollar Tree)
◆ 2 large laundry baskets
◆ 6-drawer rolling organization bin (available at stores like Walmart for about $20)
◆ Child-sized table and chairs (if budget allows)
◆ Large plastic storage tub with lid

For organizational purposes, we'll use the term "family areas" for those rooms with toys in them. There should only be three (yes, *three!*) family areas in your home when you're done—the family room itself (this is the room where the kids spend the majority of their time—it may actually be the living room, family room, or great room, depending on your floor plan); their bedroom(s); and the bathroom in which they bathe. That's it.

Now lets get started! Grab your laundry basket and go

through every room in your home that is *not* a "family area." Put every single toy you come across into your laundry basket. When your basket is full, empty it *on the floor* in your family room and continue collecting until there are only three rooms in your entire house that still have toys in them.

Bathroom

Bring your small plastic milk crate and laundry basket into the bathroom.

Put one bottle of baby wash and/or shampoo, a plastic cup for hair rinsing and a washcloth into your small milk crate.

Now add between four and six individual bath toys to the crate and place the crate somewhere out of the way, but within your child's reach, where it can live permanently—tucked in a corner, in the tub itself, or under the bathroom sink.

Put a cup on the counter with only the kids' toothbrushes and toothpaste in it. Toss all the rest of the bathroom toys and miscellaneous junk into your laundry basket, and empty it all onto the family room floor.

Child's bedroom

Bring both laundry baskets and the larger wicker basket into the bedroom.

Arrange your child's *four* favorite stuffed animals on the bed. Pile the rest on the floor.

Take all but *two* items off of the walls and ceiling. Deposit all other wall hangings and pictures in a laundry basket.

Collect all the books in the room. Choose *two* books and

place them in the wicker basket. Pile the rest of the books in a laundry basket.

Choose no more than *eight* of your child's favorite small toys and add them to the wicker basket, then add one or two self-soothing toys, like a koosh or spaghetti ball. Tuck this wicker "toy basket" on a low shelf or in a corner on the floor.

Sit down with your pile of stuffed animals and choose no more than *ten* that have serious sentimental value and arrange those on a shelf or in a toy hammock in a corner so they are not visually distracting; it does not need to be within your child's reach. Pile the remainder in a laundry basket.

Pick up all the other toys, knickknacks, wall hangings, and nifty stuff, including the junk hidden in the closet, and dump it all in the laundry baskets and haul them directly into the family room. The only toys left should be the stuffed animals in their allocated spots and the toys in the wicker basket in the corner.

Replacing patterned bedding and curtains with solid, softer hues like dusty blues, greens, and tans is a really good idea, if you can manage it. The brilliant, wildly-patterned bedding popular for kids' rooms are overstimulating even for neurotypical kids, much less our super-sensitive ones. Keeping only minimal furniture is also helpful. Adding a beanbag or body pillow can give kids somewhere to tuck into when they need some soothing sensory input. Kids who really like HBOT therapy often think a "bed tent" on a mattress on the floor is very cool, and sleep better in one than in a standard bed. (These are available on Amazon for around fifty dollars.) You may want to shop around to find one that hasn't been treated with fire retardant.

When the last pile has been hauled out, sit on the floor in the middle of the room and look around—it should be far more visually calming.

Remember that change can be hard for our kids. I found that my son was a little startled at first by his new Zen-like digs, but less upset than I'd honestly expected. He acclimated very quickly, and started seeking out his room on his own when he needed quiet time. He also had an easier time both falling and staying asleep at night. Giving children a soothing corner of the world to call their own is a gift they probably appreciate more than we may ever know.

Family room

At this point your family room will look as though there was an explosion at a toy factory. Have no fear, though, this is going to be much easier than it looks!

Collect all the "kid stuff" in the family room and pile it on the floor with the toys you've collected from all over the rest of the house.

Set your bookshelf against a wall in an area of the family room where your child can have complete access and a place to sit and work without being in a traffic pattern. A child-sized table and chair should be placed near the shelf.

Arrange your six baskets on the shelves of your bookshelf. Leave enough space on one shelf to place a medium-sized book.

Sift through the toys and choose a type of toy or activity for each of the 6 baskets. If you choose something small like wooden blocks, Little People®, or Legos®, put no more than 10 or 15 items in the basket. This number goes up for older kids and as play skills become more advanced. Simple, well-crafted toys made of unpainted wood should get preference here—they encourage more imaginative play than complex, "busy" plastic toys that require batteries, and are also less likely to contain lead and other nasty neurotoxins.

Put a 2" strip of colored tape on each basket and a corresponding piece on the edge of the shelf where the basket will sit. Puzzles and larger objects can be set out alone and labeled in the same way. This is an easy technique to help your child to learn where each item goes so they can eventually retrieve and return them on their own.

Pile all the children's books into a stack. Go through the stack quickly (this will require a fair bit of ruthlessness on your part) and deposit all those books that he or she has outgrown, hates, or that make obnoxious noises into your black trash bag. Stack only those books you feel will enrich your child's life somehow into one of the cardboard boxes. From this group, choose two of your child's favorites and place them on the bookshelf in the reserved "book spot."

With the "shelf baskets" filled and the books sorted, you'll probably still have heaps of leftover toys and other stuff spread out in front of you. This is because most kids simply have *way too many* toys to play with, which actually can prevent children—especially those on the autism spectrum, who are easily distracted and overwhelmed—from learning appropriate play skills. Odd as it may seem, significantly reducing the toy inventory will actually *benefit* your child's development.

Next, remove all craft, art, and school-supply type items (crayons, coloring books, markers, stickers, paper, chalk) from the pile, arrange them in the drawers of your rolling organization bin, and immediately roll the bin into an accessible closet. (If you don't put it away *now*, someone with little fingers will empty all the drawers you carefully organized—trust me here, I speak from experience!) Keep these "craft items" in the closet and roll them out only when needed for a project so they don't get jumbled up with the toys.

Now take all of the "skill building toys" (puzzles, blocks, stringing beads, Mr. Potato Head®, Little People, trains and tracks, legos, etc.) that *didn't* go into the shelf baskets but are still in good shape, and put them into a separate "keeper" pile. Be sure to include some that may be too advanced for your child right now. This pile should be less than half of the total toys left on the floor. If it looks like more, thin it down. Remember to be ruthless!

Stack the "keeper" toys into the second cardboard box, sorting different sets into your gallon zipper bags to simplify things when it's time to retrieve them. Tape the box shut and write "Toys For Rotation" on the outside.

Sift through the remaining toys on the floor and pull out any "baby toys" of sentimental significance that your child really doesn't play with anymore, but that you just can't bear to jettison. Tuck these "decommissioned toys" into the big plastic storage bin and write "Children's Heirlooms" on the top, and seal it shut.

Now take a deep breath and deposit *all* of the remaining toys, stuffed animals (I have no idea why it's so hard to get rid of stuffed animals), and basically *everything else left on the floor that's not broken* into your black plastic bags. Tie the bags shut and promptly put them in your car. (Really, put them in the car *now* or they will never make it out of your house. Children can sniff them out like bloodhounds and you will end up right back where you started.)

Bags in your car? Good! Now take your "Children's Heirlooms" plastic tote to the attic, basement, or some other long-term storage area. Then take your cardboard boxes—taped shut and clearly labeled "Toys for Rotation" and "Books for Rotation"—and place them in a storage area in your home that you can easily access. Sweep up all the broken toys and assorted unidentifiable plastic parts (which should be all that's left on the floor) and dump them in the trash.

When you look around the room you should now see an orderly, soothing place for your child to sit and play instead of a chaotic mess. It may seem a little spartan at first glance, but it really is a well-documented approach used worldwide by Montessori Schools to give children an opportunity to learn and grow in a serene and non-distracting environment. My son absolutely *loved* it. He was able to focus, learn appropriate play skills, and because of the simple set-up, *he actually learned to pick up after himself.* We rotate new toys from the Rotation Box onto the shelf every few weeks when the skill has been mastered or if he seems bored with an item. (Because kids with ASD are often uncomfortable with change, we usually rotate out no more than three items at a time so the shelf doesn't ever contain *only* new items.)

OK, now hop in your car and deliver your black bags to the charity of your choice. Congratulations! Today you managed to do something wonderful both for your child *and* for less fortunate kids at the same time.

When you're feeling up to it, you can try the same approach on the rest of your house—do it one room at a time. I've found that, unless you're a minimalist by nature, you can safely get rid of *half* of the junk around the house without ending up even close to bare. Besides making it easier to keep the house neat, kids really do respond to the lack of sensory overload with a reduction in meltdowns. And it provides a spectacular excuse for getting rid of those awful collectible salt & pepper shakers Great Aunt Bertha left you.

More quick and easy ways to help prevent sensory overload at home:

Ditch the fluorescents

Standard fluorescent bulbs manage to torture two senses at once by simultaneously humming and flickering. Even if you can't hear it or see it, odds are your child can. This may be a place where the energy savings just aren't worth it.

Dim the lights

60-watt bulbs are probably as high as you want to go—anything over that is too bright for our kids. Table lamps and up-lighting are far easier on the eyes than bright overhead lights.

Check your thermostat

Is it noticeably warm or cool in your house? Somewhere between 72–75° seems to be where most kids feel comfortable. While some kids with ASD are totally temperature-insensitive, many others are *hypersensitive*. Nonverbal children cannot *tell* you when they're too hot or too cold, but it *can* affect their behavior.

Toss your plug-ins, potpourris, and room sprays

Not only do they use fairly nasty chemicals that no one needs to be inhaling around the clock, they also offer way too much "olfactory input" for our kids. Don't forget to take them out of your car, too. We've found fragrance-free air neutralizers like Oust worked well if you absolutely have to use something. To *really* freshen the air, opening a window works better than anything. Even in the winter, a couple minutes a day of fresh air is worth the temperature drop incurred.

Skip the perfume and cologne

Despite the price tag or timelessness of your favorite scent, odds are it won't be appreciated by your child. I save my perfume for special occasions. (This also applies to shaving cream, moisturizers, lotions, etc. Fragrance-free is always the way to go.) It rarely occurs to us that the reason our kids shy away from some people may be simply because they find their scent overwhelming.

Kid-friendly bath products

Try to find unscented or mild naturally-scented (lavender & chamomile aren't too bad) soaps, shampoo, and wipes so your child won't be covered with a smell he finds offensive. Rainbow Research (www.rainbowresearch.com) has a great selection and lower prices than you'll find at most chain stores. They have the added advantage of being free of toxic ingredients. Most commercial "scents" are actually made from noxious chemicals that our kids are sensitive to.

Laundry

Buy your favorite laundry detergent and drier sheets in fragrance-free formulas. Or skip the dryer sheets altogether, to reduce chemical load. ASD kids generally prefer their clothes not to smell funny, and it may make getting dressed less stressful for them if they don't.

Clothing

Choose cotton or other natural fiber clothing. When buying clothes, try to stick to solid colors and those without large plastic embellishments. The loud patterns can be too visually stimulating and many kids hate the smell of the plastic designs on the front of children's shirts.

Labels

Cut the labels out of clothing if your child seems sensitive to them or they prove distracting. You may wish to write the size on the inside of each item with a fine point permanent marker to help you keep track.

Pajamas

Cotton pajamas (even a cotton t-shirt) can be a great alternative to the regular polyester kid pajamas, and may help your child sleep better. Polyester PJs, in addition to being hot and itchy, are usually treated with toxic fire-retardant chemicals.

Note: *That said, please use whatever pajamas are suggested by your government safety officials and use non-government-approved pajamas at your own risk. (In other words, please don't sue me for telling you about cotton pajamas!)*

Cleaning supplies

Many of our kids have high ammonia levels already and are sensitive to chemicals (chlorine, ammonia, phosphates, etc.) as well as the noxious odors they produce. There are some great "green" cleaners out there that are no more expensive than the old standbys. (Seventh Generation® has great kitchen cleaners and chains like Kroger's carry them.) It's also really nice to see a cleaning supply warning label that reads, *"If taken internally, drink a glass of water."*

House and lawn

Virtually all weed and insect killers smell terrible. And all it takes is one look at the results of your kid's first porphyren test (biomarkers for heavy metals and toxins) to see exactly where your bug sprays and weed killers are going. Let the dandelions grow and the insects flourish. Look at it this way—now your child will have flowers to pick for you and bugs to stick in a jar.

Bug sprays and sunscreens

Most Defeat Autism Now! (D.A.N.!) Doctors recommend that we not use DEET-based bug sprays on our kids. Kiss-my-Face's "Swyflotter®" bug spray is all natural, has a mild scent, and works well. It is also recommended that we do not use sunscreens on our children except for old-fashioned zinc—most standard SPF sunscreens use chemicals that no one needs smeared on their skin. And they block about 98% of the body's Vitamin D production. (Kids on the autism spectrum are often low in Vitamin D—it's worth having levels checked if your doctor hasn't already done so.)

Loud HVAC
Is your air conditioner of furnace loud? Ensuring that you have clean air filters and choosing a moderate temperature can keep it from cycling on and off constantly.

Dishes
If you have an automatic dishwasher, turn it on *after* your child goes to bed or when he or she is not in the house. This applies to hand washing dishes as well—the sound of clanking dishes and silverware is pretty hard on oversensitive ears. Both can contribute to meltdowns.

Phones
Many kids with ASD clap their hands over their ears when the phone rings. Set your ringer to the lowest and least obnoxious of your ring choices. This goes double for cell phones. Find a mellow ring tone and keep the volume as low as possible.

Insect/rodent deterrents
This may sound weird, but the plug-in insect and/or rodent deterrents emit a high-pitched noise many kids with ASD

can hear. There are many nontoxic kitchen herbs and spices that repel insects—an online search will yield lots of information here. If rodents are a problem, consider getting a cat.

Television

Turn the TV down until you cannot make out the words, then raise it up slowly until you can hear it comfortably. You'll usually discover that it's a lot lower than you had been listening to before. Videos are often a better alternative for our kids than television. Television, particularly those shows that are geared towards kids, are often a sensory nightmare. Cartoon characters yelling, flashing scenes, and commercials with constantly fluctuating volume levels, are simply too much visual and auditory input for our kids (or any kid for that matter) to process. The same goes for many video games. Try to make TV choices based on *sensory input as well as content.* The library or a Netflix® membership is a great way to keep from watching the same DVD over and over (and over, and over, and over…). It also allows you to avoid video stores when you're shopping with your child, which is guaranteed to produce total sensory overload—and many of the movie covers are scary for smaller children.

(If your child is early in the recovery phase, it's encouraging to know that they won't always want to watch the same one movie for the rest of their lives. As they progress, their tolerance for variety in DVDs really *does* improve!)

Music

While you may like hard rock or hiphop with heavy base, it may very likely turn your sweet child into a raging virago. If you notice a connection at your house, it's time to develop an appreciation for classical music—National Public Radio and the satellite radio carriers have a nice selection. (Mozart has actually been shown to be calming to animals.) If you just can't go there, try easy rock—the Eagles or Buffet are usually not jarring for most kids with ASD. Anything heavier should be on your MP3 player. Kid-specific music CDs may or may not be a good fit for your child. My son found some of them pretty stressful to listen to—many feature a dozen kids all singing almost together and almost in tune. Listen to them yourself *first* and then decide.

Getting Organized

Out of chaos comes order, or so claimed Nietzsche, although I'm pretty sure he didn't have a child with autism. When I think of an organized home I used to think of June Cleaver or Martha Stewart, and they are both hard acts to follow. Then I met my friend Robin. I really want to be Robin when I grow up—in addition to being supremely cool, she is living proof that with a few simple organizational changes at home a *real* mom can enjoy low stress and peace of mind.

As moms, our lives are so busy it's difficult to get our act together all at once. I found setting some reasonable goals and meeting them made it all come together in about a month. I started with (and strongly recommend) the "Multiple Calendars System" for two important reasons: first, they really *do* help things go smoother on a daily basis; and second, it makes you feel good to check things off your list!

The following techniques work for our family, but many of the moms I know use different variations on the same theme. Only you can decide what will work for you and your family.

The family organization center (otherwise known as the front of the fridge)

A couple of regularly updated calendars can bring order to the craziness we all face with appointments, therapy, meals, and extra-curricular activities. **Note:** *When mounting things on the refrigerator try 3-M Command strips instead of magnets. They're a clean way to mount larger items like calen-*

dars securely enough so they won't come crashing down when someone slams the door.

Monthly calendar. Mount a 12-month calendar on the front of your refrigerator out of reach of little hands. 8.5" x 11" is a great size. This calendar will become a lifeline for your family. Everything goes on it—therapies, doctor appointments, PTA meetings, soccer, vet appointments for the pets, everything. Update it as things come up.

Weekly calendars. Mount two smaller blank "weekly calendars," the kind with nice big squares for each day, on the front of the fridge directly below your monthly calendar. These are available as a 52-page note pad at office supply stores or you can simply print them off of your computer.

The first one should be for the week's events and appointments, and the second one is the weekly menu calendar.

With menus laid out in advance you'll be able to make an accurate grocery list which will cut the time you spend in the grocery store dramatically. (Since our kids find grocery stores stressful, the less time spent there the better.) It's also nice for the family to see what's for dinner.

Shopping list. Mount a "shopping list" notepad on your fridge next to your monthly calendar. This is used predominantly to write your weekly (yep, only once a week) grocery shopping list based on your menus. My husband has even started writing things on the list when he uses the last of something. Cool huh?

The front of your refrigerator is now a vertical "desktop." Move all the other stuff—photos, postcards, kid's art—to a bulletin board, or to the side of the fridge if it's open.

A daily schedule

When our grandmothers ran things, everything was on a schedule. In our world of fast food and soccer practice this art has somehow been lost. However, as schedules are designed to make our lives as moms easier (and our kids calmer) it may be time to make them fashionable again.

Here's a sample daily schedule—it can be modified easily to meet your family's individual needs. We posted ours on the fridge until everyone became accustomed to it.

Sample schedule

7:30 am	Breakfast
8:00 am	Supplements
12:00 noon	Lunch
1:00 pm	Nap
2:00 pm	Speech therapy
3:00 pm	Pick up kids at school
3:30 pm	Snack time and homework
4:30–5:00 pm	DVD time/Mom's break
6:00 pm	Dinner
7:30 pm	Bath time
7:55 pm	Supplements
8:00 pm	Story & bedtime
8:15–8:30 pm	Tidy up, fill in daily report
8:30–10 pm	Grownup hang-out time

Reset family areas

After tucking my son into bed I take 5–10 minutes to reset the family areas (areas with toys). This way when he putters down the stairs in the morning everything is organized and he doesn't start his day in sensory overload. I also find it nice to come downstairs ready to face the day free of yesterday's clutter.

Transition to glass

Grandma was right again—putting everything in glass jars really *was* the way to go! It turns out that plastics actually break down fairly rapidly and release toxins that many of our kids are sensitive to. (New studies reveal that chemicals like BPA are probably not all that good for *anyone*.) I took a couple of hours and replaced all the plastic bags, bottles, and boxes in the cupboards with glass jars and bottles and labeled them with masking tape. I can see exactly what I have and what I'm low on, my husband can find things in the cupboards, and my son can pick out his own snacks. And for some reason, my cupboards now stay remarkably clean. **Note:** Small jars and bottles can be purchased inexpensively at most dollar stores. For larger jars, wide mouth Mason jars (still made in the U.S. and available in several sizes) are an inexpensive way to transition to glass. Mason also sells plastic lids for the wide mouth jars so you don't have to fool around with the rings and lids— check Walmart, K-mart or your True-Value Hardware.

A shelf of their own

Find a shelf in your cupboard that can be the Official Kid Shelf. Make sure it is well within reach and stock it with sturdy jars (short and wide are safest) full of mom-approved snacks. This is a great way for them to work on self-help skills as well as expressive language—at least until they learn to open the jars themselves! My son is so proud of the fact that he can go and choose his own snack from his own cupboard. It's been a great confidence builder.

Getting records under control

A 3" 3-ring binder, a 3-hole punch, and some post-it filing tabs can make short work of the mountains of medical test results, reports, and supplement information stacked on the dining room table. Punch each report, label a tab with the test and date and stick them in the binder. I also put several extra sheets of paper in it for notes. It makes doctor's appointments a breeze, and it's great to have all the data in one place. I made additional binders for therapies and state early-intervention information as well.

Laundry helpers

If you don't already have one, you may want to pick up a 3-sectioned laundry hamper and show your kids how to use it. The first few attempts were pretty funny but now it's "big boy stuff" that we do before bath. Putting dirty laundry in the hamper is a simple confidence builder that makes one less chore for mom.

Baby gates

Installing and using baby gates religiously keeps our kids safe and us sane. I intend to use them until my son can step over them. Our grandmothers believed that there was no reason a child needed free rein of the entire house. I suspect that's how they managed to keep their houses so clean despite raising an inordinate number of children.

Mini notepad

If you don't own a Blackberry, a little spiral notepad tucked into your purse is imperative for survival; we have a lot on our plate without having to remember all the little stuff. Get in the habit of jotting things down.

Hang up

Kids in general, and our kids especially, hate it when we chat on cell phones. For us it's a balance—it's important to stay in touch with other adults, yet when using cell phones we really aren't able to give the caller or our kids our complete attention and both end up feeling a little shorted. Finding a time to dedicate to calls when our kids are otherwise engaged makes phone calls easier on everyone.

Let it ring

Growing up I was always amazed at my mother's ability to ignore a ringing phone (this was even before caller ID) when she didn't want to answer it. She would simply say, "I'm busy and I don't have time to talk to anyone right now." It's stunningly simple and totally empowering.

I cannot tell you how many times I've interrupted what I was doing, run across the house, and skidded to a stop to answer a call, only to have caller ID reveal it to be a telemarketer. Over and over I ask myself, why the crisis mode? I do not *need* to be available at all times. Before cell phones people just had to wait until I was at home to call me, and it didn't hurt my relationships with friends or family one iota. I still have to remind myself that it's OK to say, "I'm busy," let it ring, and give what I'm doing my full attention.

When I remember to do that I am honoring my own time as truly valuable. Thanks again, Mom.

Where Are We, Exactly?

The military takes global positioning very seriously for good reason. You can't very well know where you and your resources need to go if you don't know precisely where you are and where you've been. Heck, even our phones and cars have GPS to tell us our present location on the planet, complete with lat/longs. Despite all of this nifty technology, when it comes to our own kid's recovery we often feel somewhat adrift. It's extremely difficult to track progress just by looking at a child you see every day, and often our days are so busy they seem to run together. When did he stop lining things up? When was the last time he had a stomach ache? Did he stim at all yesterday? It's impossible to remember every detail. Documenting the journey in a clear and concise way has helped us provide solid data regarding the effectiveness of various treatments to his doctors, and has given us a front row seat to our son's ongoing, and to date, profound recovery.

Daily report forms. Get a 2" three-ring binder and create a daily chart to track your child's progress. Using a format with check-offs makes it fast and easy. (The easier it is to fill in, the more likely you will be to use it.) At right is the sheet I designed—you can use it as a guide to create your own, or simply copy it if you think it will meet your needs.

Making the report a part of your day. After my son is tucked in bed I tidy up the family area and take 2 minutes to fill out the report for the day. These are some things that those 2 minutes have given our family:

	Needs Improvement	Good	Excellent
Vocabulary (new sounds/word approx.)			
GI			
Appetite			
Transitions			
Sleep			
Auditory Response			
Jack Sparrow (excellent = no JS)			
Mood			
Frustration level			
Eye Contact			
Social skills			
OT skills			

Treatment

Supplements	Chelation	AIT	Home School
new: _____			

Notes: _____

Progress. Beautiful, tangible progress from day to day and week to week. It is a lovely daily reminder as to why we all work so very hard.

Closure. When we have a tough day I can fill out the daily report and let it go, because somehow putting it on paper gets it out of my head and provides a sense of closure. And that way I don't feel the need to bombard my poor unsuspecting husband with the gory details of the challenging days.

Tracking ability. Rather than guess how well a supplement or treatment is working (or not working), by instituting a "one new thing per week" policy I can track improvements, side effects, skills gained, etc. I now have clear documentation as to whether or not something is effective.

Opportunity. Specifically, the opportunity to formally document at least one positive thing about my little boy every day, even the less-than-wonderful ones. And there is always one great thing each day, if I'm actively looking for it—it reminds me to pay attention to the little miracles.

Medical records. Getting a copy of your child's full medical record and putting it in a 3-ring binder allows us as parents to see exactly where we started, how far we've come, and where we are going. Having all of the data at your disposal is empowering. We are ultimately our child's chief advocate, and since we'll end up paying for most of this out of pocket we need to be in a position to direct their care.

Funding Your Child's Recovery

Treating an Autism Spectrum Disorder is expensive and involves a truly ridiculous amount of paperwork. A good system can help keep it manageable. Here's the short course on how to do that.

Filing

Purchase a new or used filing cabinet, manila file folders, and a set of green hanging file folders. Make a file for everyone you send money to, a file for daily reports, the previous year's monthly calendar, and anything else you can think of. Put these in alphabetical order so you don't have to waste time digging. If you can find time to file once a month more power to you; some years quarterly is the very best I can do. I put the previous year's files in a plastic storage container and store it somewhere easily accessible in case I have to go back and pull files. Anything earlier I put in plastic storage containers, label the outside and tuck in the attic.

Medical receipts

Medical expenses can be tax deductible so keep your receipts. All of them! I have an 8" x 12" plastic tote with a lid (a boot box will do in a pinch) and use it to store receipts for supplements, prescriptions, treatments, therapies, etc.

401K early withdrawal

If you took money out of your 401K to pay for ASD treatments, make doubly sure to keep your receipts. If your medical expenses are substantial enough, you may be able to avoid the penalty for early withdrawal due to medical hardship.

Medical flex spending account

If you have the opportunity to put money in a flexible spending account you may want to max it out. You can't beat tax free when you have to pay out of pocket. Make sure there is no fine print in your plan that would keep you from using it for ASD treatments and make sure you use it by the end of the year if it doesn't roll over.

Get a professional to do your taxes

This will cost you around $150 and you may find it worth it to shop around. Having someone who is up to date with all the new tax regulations is crucial. We have enough on our plate without accidentally annoying the IRS. A good tax preparer will be able to help you organize all of your deductions and will save you a great deal of money and frustration in the long run. Expenses for tax preparation are also considered tax deductible.

Spend your ASD Dollar wisely

Use your resources where *you* feel it does the most good. Doctors all seem to have their own favorite treatments, therapists have another, and many parents swear by one treatment or another. It's important to remember that *you* are ultimately in charge, and *you* get to decide where you're getting the best "bang for your buck." The daily report helped us immeasurably here, because we were able to actually track what worked and what didn't. In my son's case he showed more gains after starting biomedical intervention than he had in nearly two years of speech and occupational therapies. With the data laid out in black and white, we were able to make educated financial decisions and better direct our resources.

Keeping track of household bills

With all we have to deal with every day, it's easy to lose track of time (or the bill itself) and forget to mail the electric bill when it comes due. Many moms take advantage of online bill payment to keep things from falling through the cracks. I, however, am both old-fashioned and protective of my personal data, so I still pay my bills with a check and a stamp. I've found the 31-day bill organizer (available from Lillian Vernon or Amazon) to be incredibly helpful here. I open the mail daily, recycle the heap of junk mail, and put the bill in the slot 7 days before the due date. It's also handy for remembering to mail birthday cards to elderly relatives.

Insurance

In case you didn't get the memo, Autism is considered a psychiatric disorder, at least in the eyes of most insurance companies. (Don't even get me started.) If available, a PPO plan offers you a bit more flexibility and believe me, you'll need it. For the sake of realism I'll just say "when" rather than if... *when* the insurance company denies your first claim, take the time to appeal their decision. If you're really lucky, you may find that they simply weren't provided all of the information they needed to process your claim and that the situation can be easily rectified. Also, it may be helpful to have your HR Representative contact the insurance company directly to explain your claim. If you are denied and you truly believe that under your policy it should have been covered, you may wish to contact a representative from your state's Insurance Commission. Parents of kids with ASD generally become insurance experts within the first year of diagnosis.

Season passes

Not just for football games anymore, these are now widely offered, so check to see if the places you frequent have season passes available. Many zoos and children's museums do not advertise them, but it's well worth asking. We save over a hundred dollars a year with our annual passes to the small local zoo that my animal-loving son considers his second home.

Break through therapy limbo

If your child is stuck on a waiting list for state intervention services and your family simply cannot afford speech and occupational therapies, consider getting videos. Jenny McCarthy and Sarah Clifford Scheflon, MS, CCC-SLP, developed a video series called teach2talk™ that uses video modeling to teach language development (similar to clinical speech therapy sessions). They have also developed teach2play™, a series designed to teach parents how to work with their child on purposeful play skills (similar to clinical occupational therapy sessions). These videos can get your family heading in the right direction for about $20 apiece.

Therapy materials

When buying therapy materials, you can save a bunch of money if you split the expense with another parent or two. Auditory Integration CDs like the *Listening Program* can run $250 or more, which might be too steep for an already-stretched budget. However, if a few moms all chip in and buy the set, it's a *lot* more economical. Children can begin the program sequentially; one child begins with the first CD, and when he moves to the second CD, the next child can start on the first. A third child then follows the second, until you run out of kids. Waiting a few weeks to start the program (draw straws if you want to be fair about it) is well worth the savings incurred.

Recycled toys

Shop online auctions, thrift, and consignment stores for developmental and skill-building toys. When your child has outgrown them, either sell them or pass them on to other moms. Recycling toys is a *huge* money-saver when every recovery dollar counts. It's also good for the planet.

Reinforcements

Calling in reinforcements has been around as long as anyone can remember. The Roman Legion mastered this early; their front line only fought for a specific period of time. When that time was up, a horn would sound, shields were raised, and the front line turned to the side and moved to the back of the ranks while the next line assumed their position on the front line. This ensured that the Roman front was always rested and well prepared. The Roman Legion managed to conquer most of the ancient world using this technique…if it worked for them, why not us?

I have a tendency to think I am the person best suited to care for my son on a daily basis and frankly, I probably am. Life, however, has its own tendencies, and the most notable is its unpredictability.

Which is how I found myself flat on my back and scheduled for a full hysterectomy during a period when my husband was working incredibly long hours under heavy deadlines. This situation would have been disastrous for our family had it not been for "Aunt Shelly," a gorgeous retired fashionista in Gucci sunglasses and a BMW convertible who (for reasons unknown but appreciated) ran a "hanging out with toddlers" business. Shelley had a great relationship with my son *prior* to my hospitalization, which was critical, since my son, like many kids with ASD, doesn't warm up to strangers right off the bat. It was a fantastic learning experience for me as well. Although everything wasn't done "my way," they did wonderfully together on their own, and had grand adventures along the way.

Because we never know what life is going to throw at us, it's good to line up our reinforcements well in advance of emergencies.

Double up
Make sure that there are at least two people other than your-self (and not including your spouse) who can manage your child—this means meals, supplements, schedules—the whole nine yards.

Share your system
It is extremely comforting to ensure that someone else knows your organizational systems. Having your medical data, daily reports and financial systems in place make it easier for someone to step in, but it is our responsibility to let someone else know how it all works. It's awfully nice to know that if our appendix bursts the mortgage will still get paid and our kid's progress will still be tracked.

Prepare kids in advance
The first time your child is out of your personal care shouldn't be when you end up in the hospital with a bro-ken leg! If you're the primary caretaker, try to leave your child in someone else's care for a few hours every month, so your child gets comfortable with the idea.

Finding the Right Sitter

A good sitter is an imperative key to our sanity and our child's socialization. Finding the right sitter for our kids can be a scary undertaking, particularly if, like mine, your child is nonverbal. Finding a responsible and trustworthy candidate is crucial to our peace of mind.

Family

Take family members up on their offers to baby-sit—they wouldn't have offered if they weren't serious. Family sitters are often easiest to transition to for our kids since there is usually a preexisting relationship.

Universities

No family nearby? Check to see if your local university has an early education program. Often students studying early/elementary education and special needs education will jump at the chance to work with children with ASD. These same students often have previous experience with special needs kids. Most universities have a job listing board on campus or on the web where you can spell out your requirements and job details.

Agencies and online placement services

There are agencies and online services that will help you locate the right sitter or nanny for your family. Check the fees involved in using the services, make sure that the person has the experience you are looking for, and that you are not under any sort of obligation should the sitter not be a good fit. In addition, ensure that they do background investigations and ask for a copy if you are considering hiring someone.

Schools

Check with your local school system—they may have a list of substitute teachers who are interested in working with families.

Easy background checks

When you find a candidate you like, ask for permission to do a background check. With a little bit of personal data and $30–$60 you can go online and find out if this person has a record. Go to *MySpace* and see what persona they show to the rest of the world. You may find out that their "habits" are not conducive to your family. Awful as it sounds, don't forget to check the sex offenders database and child abuse registries in your state. If you are not comfortable and/or don't have time to do it on your own, there are many online services (such as nannybackgrounds.com) that will run all of the checks for you for a fee. If it's important to you, feel free to request a drug test.

Check references

Very few people actually do this but it is well worth the few minutes on the phone. Often it helps you gain a great deal of insight and I have found that previous employers (usually other moms) can offer you a wealth of information.

Conduct interviews

Interview your top two or three choices. Have a list of questions and criteria prepared and decide in advance on which items you're willing to be flexible. There are some great "interview question lists" online if you need somewhere to start. Part of the interview should entail meeting your child and observing how well they work together. Keep in mind that our kids are not often great fans of "new," so try to look past the initial reaction and go for overall compatibility.

Trust your instincts

This is no place for political correctness. Trust your instincts—you have to do what you are most comfortable with no matter *what* the political implications. While I'm sure there are many wonderful male sitters out there, because my son is currently nonverbal, I choose to hire only women. While I'm well aware that it is innately sexist, it's a personal choice that I'm comfortable with.

Help them to help you

Have your list of numbers, specific instructions (food, supplements, etc.) and house rules ready *before* the sitter arrives. Take time to address any questions or concerns they have in advance.

The test run

I always do a two-hour test run for a new sitter. When the sitter arrives I disappear. I work in the garden, or hide with a book on the porch. That way I'm there as a safety net while they get to know one another. At the end of a test run

I schedule an additional half-hour to address any questions or concerns that she may have.

Calling
If you need to call home while the sitter is there, try to call at a time when you won't disrupt the schedule. Talk to your child only if you and the sitter agree it is a good idea. Often talking to us may set our children off, forcing the sitter to start the "mommy detox" process all over again.

Get home on time
Just as we expect the sitter to arrive on time, we also have an obligation to return home on time. Their time is just as valuable as ours and this show of respect will go a long way in helping to sustain a long-term relationship. Remember, a great sitter always has other opportunities available to them.

Debriefing
Schedule five minutes of debriefing time when you return. Find out how their time together went. Address any concerns or questions and schedule the next appointment. It's a good idea to ask your child how he or she thinks it went, as well.

Notes

CHAPTER TWO

Feeding the Troops

Supplements

Not too many years ago, autism was considered a mental disorder, and all treatment was based on that premise. Today, autism spectrum disorders are generally understood to be much more complex, and thousands of parents have found nutritional supplementation beneficial to their children. For parents of newly diagnosed kids, the world of nutritional supplements can be a little overwhelming.

Supplements usually fall into three basic categories—*vitamins and minerals* to support the immune system, *digestive supplements* such as probiotics and enzymes to help with digestive problems, and *amino acids*, which support brain function. A D.A.N.! doctor, or any doctor with experience in treating autism, can give you a comprehensive list of supplements to try.

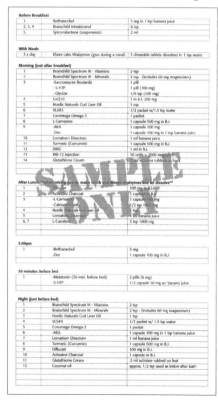

Before Breakfast			
1		Bethanechol	5 mg in 1 tsp banana juice
2, 3, 4		Brainchild Intestinend	6 tsp
5		Spironolactone (suspension)	2 ml

With Meals			
5 x day		Klaire Labs Vitalzymes (give during a meal)	3 chewable tablets dissolved in 1 tsp water

Morning (just after breakfast)			
1		Brainchild Spectrum III - Vitamins	2 tsp
2		Brainchild Spectrum III - Minerals	2 tsp - (includes 60 mg magnesium)
3		-Saccromyces Boulardii	1 pill
		- 5-HTP	1 pill (100 mg)
		- Glycine	1/8 tsp (500 mg)
4		CoQ10	1 in B.J. 200 mg
5		Nordic Naturals Cod Liver Oil	1 tsp
6		VLS#3	1/2 capsule w/1.5 tsp water
7		Coromega Omega-3	1 packet
8		L-Carnosine	1 capsule 500 mg in B.J.
9		-AKA	1 capsule 100 mg
		-Zinc	1 capsule 100 mg in 1 tsp banana juice
10		Lomatium Disectum	1 ml banana juice
11		Turmeric (Curcumin)	1 capsule 500 mg in B.J.
12		DMG	1 ml in B.J.
13		MB-12 Injection	10 units = 2500 mcg
14		Glutathione Cream	mixer rubbed on back

After Lunch			
1		-Cod Liver	100 mg in B.J.
2		-Activated Charcoal	1 capsule in B.J.
3		-L-Carnosine	1 capsule 500 mg
		-Calcium Citrate	1/2 tsp 1000 mg
4		Nordic Naturals Cod Liver Oil	1 tsp
5		Lomatium Disectum	1 ml banana juice
6, 7		L-Carnitine	3 tsp 1000 mg

5:00pm			
1		-Bethanechol	5 mg
		-Zinc	1 capsule 100 mg in B.J.

30 minutes before bed			
1		-Melatonin (30 min. before bed)	2 pills (6 mg)
		-5-HTP	1/2 capsule 50 mg w/ banana juice

Night (just before bed)			
1		Brainchild Spectrum III - Vitamins	2 tsp
2		Brainchild Spectrum III - Minerals	2 tsp - (includes 60 mg magnesium)
3		Nordic Naturals Cod Liver Oil	1 tsp
4		VLS#3	1/2 packet w/ 1.5 tsp water
5		Coromega Omega-3	1 packet
6		-AKA	1 capsule 100 mg in 1 tsp banana juice
7		Lomatium Disectum	1 ml banana juice
8		Turmeric (Curcumin)	1 capsule 500 mg in B.J.
9		Diflucan	100 mg in B.J.
10		Activated Charcoal	1 capsule in B.J.
11		Glutathione Cream	.5 ml w/mixer rubbed on feet
12		Coconut oil	approx. 1/2 tsp used as lotion after bath

Most of our kids take more nutritional supplements in a day than your average Olympic athlete. Here are some suggestions that other moms have passed along to keep track of them all.

Supplement list

Maintain a "current supplements list" (we use a MS Word table) and keep a copy folded in your wallet. In addition, we print an 8.5" x 11" copy and laminate it. That one stays with the supplements. Leave a few blank lines so you can add to it without having to go to your computer each time.

Dedicate space

We have three areas dedicated to supplements:

◆ A shelf on the door of the refrigerator for liquids and probiotics

◆ An 18" area of counter space dedicated exclusively to preparation and storage of daily supplements. We use a rectangular wire basket to keep them all contained yet visible. Write the name of each supplement on its cap in indelible ink for easy identification.

◆ A large kitchen drawer for supplements not used daily or "extras." It's generally cheaper to buy multiples and/or order with a couple other moms to save on shipping

Preparation

If your child can swallow pills you're in great shape! My friend Annette sets up small Dixie cups every Sunday (at least two for each day of the week, since morning and evening supplements are often different) and fills them with the following week's supplements. She then labels zipper bags (Monday AM, Monday PM, etc.) and transfers the supplements to their appropriate bags. Using this technique allows her to get all the supplements sorted on her day off so she can just grab them and go during the week when things are busy.

Magic Potions

You'll need:

- Pill crusher (available at Dollar Tree or a drug store
- Juice (pineapple or banana juice works well)
- Small jar with wide mouth
- 2 tsp oral syringes with caps (available at any pharmacy—a bag of 100 costs around twenty dollars and can be rinsed and reused multiple times)

Open the capsule or grind up the tablet. Pour powder into your jar, add two teaspoons of juice, and stir. Tilt the jar, dip the syringe into the juice and pull out the plunger slowly to draw in the mixture. Put a cap on the syringe, lay it on the counter, and repeat the process as many times as needed. (Some supplements can be combined to reduce the total number of potions.) Liquid supplements can be drawn right into a syringe as well; it's less messy than a spoon.

My son doesn't know how to swallow pills yet, so we use liquid supplements where available and make "magic potions" out of the tablets and capsules.

Although potions are mixed daily, they can be prepared several hours in advance. I always assemble and bag any lunchtime potions when I'm making the morning ones so I can just grab them on my way out the door if we won't be home for lunch.

On a final note: Most nutritional supplements taste OK and tend not to have side effects, but it's a good idea to try them yourself before introducing them to your child, especially if he or she is non-verbal. Cod liver oil is probably the least palatable, but mixing it well with pineapple juice helps mask the fishy flavor.

Getting your child to take supplements

This takes time, a sense of humor, and honesty. Making the supplements a part of the daily schedule, and really sticking to it, helps a lot. Although the first few efforts may be difficult, making a game out of squirting the "magic potions" into your child's mouth (which doesn't need to be open for it to work, by the way) will also make things easier.

We always explain to our son in simple terms what each supplement is for ("this one will help your brain work better, this one will make you see better, and *this* one will make your bones strong") and why it's important that he take them every day. Some, like the Vitamin MB-12 shot, obviously make him feel good—he actually brings it to my attention if I'm late with his MB-12 shot!

Choosing supplements

Many doctors will give you an extensive list of supplements, and these lists can change with differing lab results over time. It became our policy to introduce only one new supplement each week. Originally, in our excitement, we'd start several at once, but we soon realized that when we saw significant improvement we couldn't pinpoint *which* supplement had made the difference. And when his stomach was upset we didn't know which one didn't agree with him. Though slower, adding only one supplement at a time allowed us to track what was working and what wasn't.

As with most things, everyone has their own favorite brand of supplements. I know many doctors (as well as other moms) who have *very* strong preferences. Here are some things to consider when choosing supplements:

1. Price. Treating ASD is expensive, and it's important to be realistic. If you simply can't afford the most expensive probiotics, less-expensive ones are far better than none at all.

2. Ingredients. When it comes to ingredients, the fewer inactive ingredients (fillers) the better.

3. Country of origin. It's wise to avoid countries with poor safety records. Call the company if you want to know the source.

4. Availability. Is it available locally, can it be ordered online, does it need to be made at a compounding pharmacy, or do you need to order it through a doctor? These are all important factors to consider. (Klaire Labs and Metagenics products are only available through physicians, for example.)

5. Palatability. Can you get your child to take it? The best brand means nothing if it tastes awful and your kid spits it out.

Thinking "outside the box" can help. Bodybuilders have used L-Carnitine for decades and it's available through those outlets at a reasonable price in all-natural raspberry flavored liquid form. Getting 1000 mg of bitter vitamin C powder into a small child can be daunting until you realize that you can buy adult strength (250 mg) all-natural Vitamin C gummies, and almost any kid will cheerfully eat four of them. In fact, they make great "rewards" for being a good sport about taking supplements! A little creativity goes a long way.

Basic Training

Remember the scene in *A Christmas Story* where the mother makes pig sounds in a desperate attempt to get Randy to eat? Welcome to our world. I have beautiful, albeit bygone, memories of my son eating Thai food, happily trying everything on his plate and mine, too. We may well get back there, but alas, time takes time.

We all know that you are what you eat, but getting children with ASD to eat is often a time-consuming and fairly exhausting experience. Here are a few tips (and a few recipes) to help things along.

Check zinc levels

A lot of kids on the spectrum are zinc-deficient. And a lot of people, including doctors, don't seem to know that a zinc deficiency can simply be a result of taking calcium supplements, because calcium inhibits the body's ability to absorb zinc. (*Anyone* who takes calcium supplements should probably consider adding a zinc supplement as well.) *Oddly, one of the common symptoms of a zinc deficiency is that it negatively affects the sense of taste.* Within days of starting on a zinc supplement, my son started eating things he hadn't touched in years, with little or no prompting on our part.

Probiotics

The good flora that helps repair the gut and rebuild the immune system can also make a huge difference in our kids' eating patterns. Think about it—if virtually everything you ate gave you a terrible stomach ache, you'd be suspicious of food, too.

The GF/CF diet

A lot of new Autism Moms are confused with this whole "gluten-free/casein free diet" they keep hearing about, including what GF/CF actually means.

They wonder: What is it? Does it work? Is it safe? There are a lot of good books on the subject, but here's the short course:

Gluten is a protein found in wheat and casein in dairy products. Being "gluten free/casein free" simply means that wheat, i.e., flour, and dairy products are removed from the diet.

Does it work? Well, a *huge* number of parents swear that a gluten-free, casein-free diet has done more to help their ASD child than anything else, and although there are no random controlled double-blind studies to back it up (you can't really *do* a double-blind study with food unless everyone is blindfolded), it's pretty unlikely that they could all be mistaken!

The fact that other parents have not had as much success could be explained by a couple things. First is that ASD is a pretty big tent, and may have several different underlying causes resulting in the same symptoms. If a child has no problems digesting gluten or casein, removing it from his diet probably won't do much. Second is that a GF/CF diet is an "all-or-nothing proposition"—90% GF/CF is really no different than not removing any gluten or casein at all. If you are going to try it, you have to make a real commitment.

It's been noticed that the kids who seem to crave bread, crackers, and milk, and practically live on those things alone, respond best to a GF/CF diet. (These are often the kids with gastrointestinal problems.) The theory here is that in these kids, gluten and casein molecules called peptides attach to the opioid receptors (think opium here) in the brain, and act as a drug. Removing gluten and casein makes these kids less "foggy."

What about safety? Many mainstream pediatricians who are unfamiliar with the GF/CF diet worry that it may cause nutritional deficiencies, and this can scare parents away from trying something that may be of great benefit to their child. Although the GF/CF diet removes one source of calcium from the diet, it's important to remember that dairy products are only *one* source of calcium (a cup of collard greens has more calcium than a cup of milk) and a lot of the world consumes a lot less milk and wheat than we do with no ill effects at all. Japan, for example, eats a primarily rice-based diet and consumes a lot less milk, and the Japanese boasts both the world's lowest infant mortality rate *and* a longer life expectancy than America.

And if for some strange reason you can't get your kid to eat collard greens, an 800 mg calcium supplement will cover the daily requirements for a 4–8 year old.

Run peptide tests

A simple $60 peptide urine test will tell you if your child is sensitive to gluten or casein. If your child's gluten and casein peptides are elevated, the gluten-free casein-free (usually referred to as GF/CF) diet will probably be well-worth the work involved. If your child's peptides are OK, but histamine levels are high (which was the case with my son), the GF/CF diet may also work wonders.

Note: Many kids have elevated gluten and casein peptides in the early period of their recovery. Later, when the gut is healed, some of them can transition back to a regular diet, while others remain sensitive.

Keeping your child gluten and casein free

GFCF diets can be hard to maintain if your child attends school or daycare. Discuss the diet with staff and explain what changes you will be making and what they can do to help. "A Gluten Free/Casein Free Kid" T-shirt as well as GF/CF labels on both lunchbox and backpack can help remind teachers and caregivers.

Packaged vs homemade

Every day there is more and more GF/CF prepared food becoming available; unfortunately, it can be expensive and may not meet your child's taste requirements. In fact, one bite of a commercial GF/CF chocolate chip cookie is enough to convince most people the diet will never work! One of the easiest (and cheapest) ways to go GF/CF is to cook from scratch. There are some great cookbooks available and many websites and organic markets where you can buy ingredients. Even if you are not Rachel Ray, odds are the food you make will taste a lot better than the stuff you buy in packages. And you won't have to take out a second mortgage on your house to pay for it.

Dietary enzymes

These are natural enzymes that help break down gluten, casein, fats, and pretty much anything else you can think of. Many families, because of prohibitive costs or because their child would rather go hungry than eat a GF/CF diet (I heard a kid once define gluten and casein as "that stuff that makes food taste good") use dietary enzymes instead of, or in conjunction with, a GF/CF Diet.

If your child is on a GF/CF diet and in school or daycare (or any situation in which you don't have 100% food control), daily enzymes are good "insurance." Houston Labs Peptizyme and Klair Labs Vitalzymes (Klaire labs products must be ordered through a physician) are two commonly used enzymes. A great deal of information is available on-line; you can contact other parents for advice at www.enzymestuff.com.

Artificial flavors and colors

Back in the early 1980s, my little brother was part of the "first wave" of ADD/ADHD kids to start turning up.

Rather than putting him on Ritalin®, which was just starting to gain popularity back then, my parents kept him on the Feingold Diet, which worked a lot better, and without any of Ritalin's side effects. I actually *grew up* with Tom's Toothpaste®—it's all we ever used in our house. (Luckily, they have more flavors now.) And my mom made Jell-O® from scratch, just like I do for my son.

Thirty years after Dr. Feingold's book on the subject was first published, the American Academy of Pediatrics finally admitted that they (gasp)*"were wrong,"* and artificial flavors and colors can cause hyperactivity, attention difficulties, and other behavioral problems in children. Needless to say, this was not much of a surprise to me.

Checking food labels and rejecting anything with artificial flavors, colors, and/or phenols (this applies to over-the-counter drugs containing acetaminophenol also) in its ingredients list is an inexpensive and simple way to help our kids. Many kids on the autism spectrum also have hyperactivity and/or attention deficit issues to deal with on top of the sensory ones.

Lendon Smith and Ben Feingold were two of the earliest pioneers in treating children's health and behavior problems with nutritional intervention rather than pharmaceuticals, and their books on the subject are still worth tracking down.

Buying safer food
Buying produce at your local farmers' market is a great way to get fresh food while supporting local farmers. Even if they are not "certified organic," small farms need to use far less in the way of pesticides than the huge commercial farms, and practice a greener form of agriculture that's good for the planet.

Wash up
A $3 bottle of Organic Fruit & Vegetable Wash can help remove pesticides and bacteria from food if organic produce is simply out of your family budget.

Grow your own

During WWII every American family dug up part of their lawn and planted a Victory Garden—Eleanor Roosevelt even had one on the White House lawn! It's cheap food, good exercise, and an absolute blast for the kids. Dig up a 5' x 5' chunk of lawn, or pick up some pots and do some container gardening. Plant some things that are easy to grow, such as strawberries, tomatoes, squash, pumpkins, cucumbers, lettuce, and sunflowers for the bird feeder— whatever sounds like fun. My son loves watering the garden, and ambles out to his strawberry patch every time he needs a snack in the summer.

Try freeze-dried

Often when my son wouldn't eat a fruit or vegetable for love or money, it was not so much the taste as the *texture* (back to that sensory stuff) that bothered him. We discovered freeze-dried fruits and vegetables were a great alternative to fresh. Rather than buy the expensive little bags at the grocery store, we go to www.emergencyessentials.com. They sell a huge variety of freeze-dried fruits and vegetables in coffee-can-sized portions for a far better price. To maintain crispness, once we open a can we transfer the contents and the silica packs into a gallon zipper bag, put it back in the can, and store it in a cool dry place.

Weekly menu

After reading Getting Organized in Chapter 1 you will hopefully have a weekly menu in place. Using a weekly menu can help prepare our kids for mealtimes. There is far less arguing over food when everyone knows what we are having for dinner in advance.

Schedule family meals (and eat them at the table!)

Scheduling meals for the same time each day and sitting down as a family to eat those meals can make a huge difference in our kids' eating habits. We've found that my son is far more likely to try something on his plate if everyone around him is eating it as well.

Organic options

Organic food, grown without pesticides and chemical fertilizers, is wonderful. However, you may come across a few obstacles in the world of prepared organics… the first is that it's often not particularly "kid-friendly"! I know very few four-year-olds who think flaxseed wheatgrass bread with cacao nibs is worth eating. There are a few companies now producing *real* kid food, but they are really a minority

Another obstacle is availability—in many rural areas it's still difficult to get a wide variety of organics at reasonable prices. You may want to check and see if there is a whole foods cooperative in your area. You can also ask your local grocery store to carry certain items you purchase regularly, or find online markets for non-perishables with low shipping fees (if you order with other moms you may be able to save on shipping).

Prices for organics can be prohibitive so it pays to shop around. Many stores have their own less expensive "house brand" organics. When buying chicken, rather than buying organic free-range (which runs at least $7 per pound),

I buy "hormone & antibiotic free." Food Lion and Tyson both market this. Teresa Holler's excellent book, *Holler For Your Health*, is a great guide for figuring out where organic really counts.

Consider wild game

If you have a hunter in your family, it's worth remembering that "wild" red meats like venison and elk (and wild poultry like pheasant and quail) are about as organic as you can get. If you have no experience with game, have it ground into hamburger, and freeze it in one-pound packages. Ground venison is indistinguishable in things like meatballs and spaghetti sauce, except that it's leaner and you may need to add a touch of oil.

Cooking from scratch

Few people learn to cook from scratch anymore, but don't let that intimidate you—*anyone* can learn to cook! It's a lot easier than you think, far less expensive than buying prepared food, and you have total control of ingredients. The easiest way to start is to go buy an old *Betty Crocker's Cookbook* (at least 30 years old) written in the days before the invention of take-out and microwaves, when whole ingredients were all that was available, and women *had* to learn to cook in order to feed their families. You can find them on Amazon, at used book stores, and at thrift stores. Betty, bless her heart, always dedicated a chapter to bringing novices up to speed. In addition to "made-from-scratch" recipes, most of her cookbooks also define terms, give basic instruction, contain conversion charts, and have very easy-to-use glossaries.

Put your kids to work

Get a step-stool and get them to work in the kitchen. Though at first uninterested, my son is now a baking *fanatic*. He slides his step-stool to the counter and sidles up to help as soon as he sees me starting to cook. You can learn together, read recipes, sift, mix, measure, roll and pour. It's a great opportunity for them to master skills and build confidence. My little guy is also far more inclined to try something new if he helped cook it. It's also a lot of fun to see him realize he can now *make* his favorite foods—his first pumpkin pie was a very big deal.

Recipes

Here are some of my little guy's favorite "kid helper" recipes. I use primarily organic ingredients (many of which you can buy bulk at whole foods co-ops), which are far less expensive than prepackaged organic food. Experiment, modify and most of all, have fun!

French Toast

3 eggs
1/4 cup rice milk
Dash of cinnamon
2 slices of GFCF bread

Whisk eggs, milk, and cinnamon together in a large shallow dish. Cut each bread slice in half, and place the 4 halves into the mixture. Let it soak until the side is well covered, then flip carefully and soak other side. Heat greased pan or griddle on low flame. Using a spatula, carefully place French toast on pan and cover. Check frequently and turn when golden. Cook opposite side until golden and drizzle with real maple syrup or honey. (If you want to use butter, clarify it first to remove the casein.)

The Best Chicken Strips Ever

Because you're working with hot grease here, these are best made after little ones are in bed. You can make piles of strips at once and freeze them for quick and easy dinners later on.

Note: If your kid is a chicken strip junkie like mine, it's well worth the money to invest in a FryDaddy® (about $30 from Amazon). Keeping oil at a constant temperature on your stove can be difficult, but a cast iron Dutch oven is probably the best bet there.

4 eggs
1/4 cup water or rice milk (I usually use water)
4 cups GF flour (I use a rice flour/garbanzo flour mix)
2 teaspoons salt
Pepper to taste
Garlic powder to taste
4–6 cups vegetable oil or lard (amount depends on what you are cooking it in—the fat needs to be at least 3" deep in pan)
Several pounds of (antibiotic/hormone free) chicken breasts

Get yourself a frying thermometer if you are using the stovetop method. Maintaining 360 degrees is your goal—too hot and the inside won't cook properly; too cold and food gets greasy. Really, unless you're from the Deep South, where frying great chicken is an art passed on from generation to generation, invest in the FryDaddy—it'll save you a lot of aggravation. (It also makes great homemade French fries.) And no, a crock pot won't work; it doesn't get hot enough.

Cover work area with wax paper to contain the floury mess and turn on the exhaust fan in the kitchen before you start.

Whisk eggs and water together in a shallow pan (cake pans work well). Mix flour, salt, pepper and garlic together in another shallow pan. Place side by side. Slice chicken into 1–2" slices and set in shallow pan.

Cover cookie sheet with 3 layers of paper towels and place within reach but well away from stove.

Heat oil or lard to 360 degrees over medium heat in Dutch oven on stove or plug in the FryDaddy.

In groups of 4 pieces, dip chicken in flour mixture, shake off, dip in egg mixture, then dip back in to flour mixture. To make them super-crispy, I dip them in egg and flour a second time.

Shake off excess flour gently over flour pan and place strips carefully in hot oil (tongs work great for this). When the bottoms turn golden, flip and allow the other side to cook. While the first ones are in the fryer prepare four more pieces. When strips are crispy and golden brown carefully remove from oil and place on cookie sheet to drain. Repeat ad infinitum.

When strips have cooled, remove paper towels and place cookie sheet in freezer.

After 1–2 hours transfer chicken strips to gallon freezer bags.

To reheat: Place on cookie sheet in preheated oven at 400 degrees for 5–10 minutes so they stay crispy. In a pinch, they can be microwaved, but they won't be as crispy.

Spaghetti & Meatballs

Meatballs

1 lb ground beef or venison (antibiotic/hormone free)
2/3 cup crushed Rice Chex®
1/4 cup rice milk
1 teaspoon salt
1 teaspoon Worcestershire sauce (Leah and Perrin's is gluten-free)
1/4 teaspoon pepper
1 clove crushed garlic or 1 teaspoon garlic powder
1/2 teaspoon oregano
1/2 teaspoon basil
1 small onion, diced
2 eggs

Mix all ingredients, roll into 1½" balls (good kid job) and bake in 400 degree oven for 20 minutes or cook over medium heat on stovetop for 15 minutes. Gently turn meatballs as needed.

While meatballs are cooking, prepare your sauce.

Sauce

(Organic sauce in a jar works just fine, too. Check to make sure it's GF)
1 small onion (chopped)
2 cloves of garlic crushed or chopped (garlic powder works fine, too)
1–2 tablespoons olive oil
1 small can organic tomato paste
2–4 cups water (start with 2 cups and add water until sauce is the consistency you prefer)

Diced tomatoes (canned or fresh)

Mushrooms (washed and sliced)

Chopped zucchini, carrots, or whatever you feel like adding

1/2 teaspoon oregano

1/2 teaspoon basil

1/2 teaspoon marjoram (not required)

Salt to taste

Pepper to taste

1 package GF/CF spaghetti

In a large pot (you will be adding your meatballs to this eventually), sauté oil, onions and garlic over medium high heat. When onions become opaque, lower heat to medium and add your other ingredients. Add 2 cups water and continue to add water until it reaches the consistency and flavor your family prefers (remember that the vegetables will release some water as they cook as well). When sauce begins to boil, lower heat and allow to simmer.

When meatballs are done gently place them into your sauce. Continue to simmer at very low heat. You may want to cover the pot loosely to prevent splatters.

Put pot of water on to boil for spaghetti. Try to time spaghetti for 10 minutes after the meatballs are done. This will give you time to simmer your meatballs in your sauce while the spaghetti is cooking.

Meatloaf

1½ lbs of ground beef

3 slices of GF/CF bread torn into tiny pieces or
½ cup crushed Rice Chex®

2 eggs

1 cup rice milk

1 small onion diced (about 1/4 cup)

1 tablespoon Lea & Perrin's® Worcestershire sauce

1 teaspoon salt

1 teaspoon mustard

1/4 teaspoon pepper

1/4 teaspoon rubbed sage

1/4 teaspoon garlic powder

1/2 cup catsup or BBQ Sauce (check for gluten!)

Preheat oven to 350 degrees

Mix all ingredients except catsup or BBQ sauce. Shape mixture in ungreased loaf pan (approx. 8 x 4 x 2"), spoon catsup or BBQ sauce over top and bake uncovered for 1 to 1¼ hours.

"I Can't Believe It's GFCF" Bread

Yes, you really can bake bread…!

This bread is soft and white, smells wonderful baking, and tastes like "real bread." It's great for PB&J sandwiches.

The foundation of this recipe is Bette Hagman's Basic Featherlight Rice Bread. I made changes necessary to make it casein free as well. If you are interested in GFCF I would highly recommend purchasing Bette Hagman's books, *The Gluten Free Gourmet Bakes Bread* and *The Gluten Free Gourmet Makes Dessert.* Her recipes are fantastic and can be made casein free with a few easy adjustments.

It looks complicated but don't let it fool you. This is a very simple recipe, once you have all the ingredients together you'll find it takes only two bowls, four minutes of mixing and a quick rise.

Bette Hagman's Featherlight Rice Flour Mix (cornstarch free)
(makes 9 cups)

3 cups white rice flour
3 cups tapioca flour
3 cups arrowroot flour
3 tablespoons potato flour (not starch)

Mix the flours well & store in a zipper bag or jar.

Here we go….

Grease medium-sized bread pan and dust with rice flour mix.

Dry Ingredients

3 cups Featherlight Rice Flour Mix

2¼ teaspoons xantham gum

1½ teaspoons unflavored gelatin

1½ teaspoons egg replacer (made by Ener-G®)

1 teaspoon salt

3 tablespoons sugar

1/3 cup almond meal

2¼ teaspoons dry yeast

In a large bowl, mix the dry ingredients and set aside.

Wet Ingredients

1 egg (room temperature)

2 egg whites (room temperature. Reconstituted powdered egg whites work fine)

4½ tablespoons coconut oil

3/4 teaspoon vinegar

1 tablespoon honey

1½ cups warm water

In a large bowl mix all wet ingredients except the water with an electric mixer until blended. Add warm water and mix carefully until blended.

With mixer set to low, add dry ingredients slowly, scraping the bowl occasionally until blended.

Mix on high speed for 3½ minutes.

Pour into prepared loaf pan.

Cover with plastic wrap and drape a dish towel over the top. Set in a warm place to rise for 35–60 minutes (35 minutes for rapid rise yeast, 60 minutes for regular) until the center of the dough is flush with the top of the pan. If you let it rise past the top of the pan the center will sink as the baked loaf cools. It tastes fine but just isn't as pretty.

Bake in a preheated 400 degree oven for 10 minutes, then cover loosely with tinfoil (without taking it out of oven) and continue baking for another 45–50 minutes.

You can brush the top with ghee or coconut oil after it has been cooling for 5 minutes. Let it cool completely in the pan and store in a zipper bag.

Sweet Stuff

Knox Blox (all natural gelatin jigglers)

4 envelopes Knox Unflavored Gelatin
1 cup cold fruit juice (grape, cherry, apple, and raspberry work best)
3 cups fruit juice, heated to boiling
2 tablespoons sugar (optional)

Sprinkle gelatin over cold juice in large bowl; let stand 1 minute. Add hot juice and stir until gelatin completely dissolves, about 5 minutes. Stir in sugar. Pour into 13 x 9 x 2" pan.

Refrigerate until firm, about 3 hours. Cut into 3" squares.

GF/CF Sweet Snack Mix

1/2 cup coconut oil
1/2 cup sugar
1 heaping teaspoon cinnamon
1/2 teaspoon ground ginger (optional)
9 cups Rice Chex
1 cup raisins
1 cup dried apple slices
1/2 cup diced crystallized ginger (optional)

Preheat oven to 250 degrees.

Melt coconut oil in microwave. Mix sugar, cinnamon, and ground ginger in small bowl. If you have a shaker, pour the cinnamon sugar mix into it for easier sprinkling.

Pour Rice Chex into a really big bowl and drizzle coconut oil over it. Sprinkle cinnamon sugar over Chex and mix well. Spread onto 2 cookie sheets or jellyroll pans and bake 1 hour, stirring every 15 minutes.

Pour hot Chex back into bowl. Add raisins, apples, and crystallized ginger Stir well. Spread on cookie sheets to cool completely. When cool, store in jars or Ziploc bags.

Pumpkin bread

2½ cups sugar (can be dropped to 2 cups)
2/3 cup vegetable oil
4 eggs
1 can pumpkin
2/3 cup water
3⅓ cups GF flour
1½ teaspoons xantham gum
2 teaspoons baking soda
1½ teaspoons salt
1 teaspoon cinnamon
1 teaspoon ground cloves
1/2 teaspoon baking powder
1/2 cup chopped nuts, dates or both (optional)

Preheat oven to 350 degrees. Grease bottoms of 2 large loaf pans. In large bowl mix sugar, oil eggs, pumpkin and water. Stir in remaining ingredients. Pour into pans and bake until wooden toothpick inserted in center comes out clean (approximately 1 hour, 10 minutes). Cool slightly and loosen sides of pan. Remove from pans and cool on racks. These freeze well, too.

Gingerbread

2⅓ cups GF flour
1½ teaspoons xantham gum
1/3 cup sugar
1/2 cup shortening
1 cup molasses
3/4 cup hot water
1 teaspoon baking soda
1 teaspoon ground ginger
1 teaspoon cinnamon
3/4 teaspoon salt
1 egg

Preheat oven to 325 degrees. Grease and flour square pan (9 x 9 x 2"). Beat all ingredients on low speed, scraping bowl constantly, for 30 seconds. Beat on medium speed for 3 minutes. Pour into pan and bake until wooden toothpick inserted into center comes out clean, about 50 minutes.

Brownies

1 cup sugar

1/2 cup shortening

1 teaspoon GF vanilla (optional)

2 eggs

2/3 cup GF flour

1 teaspoon xantham gum

1/2 cup cocoa powder

1/2 teaspoon baking powder

1/4 teaspoon salt

1/2 cup nuts or chocolate chips (optional)

Preheat oven to 350 degrees. Grease square 9 x 9 x 2-inch pan. Mix sugar, shortening, vanilla and eggs in large bowl. Stir in remaining ingredients (except nuts or chocolate chips). Once mixed, stir in nuts and/or chips.

Spread batter in pan and bake until toothpick inserted into center comes out clean, approximately 20–25 minutes.

GF/CF Excellent Thanksgiving Pumpkin Pie

(The whole family will enjoy this pie!)

To make crust, mix:

8-ounce package crushed GF/CF gingersnaps

4 tablespoons melted coconut oil

Press into bottom of pie pan and up sides

In large mixing bowl, combine:

4 eggs

½ cup melted shortening or coconut oil

Add:

3 cups canned pumpkin (not pumpkin pie mix!)

1 cup brown sugar

½ cup white sugar

1 teaspoon salt

1 teaspoon cinnamon

½ teaspoon ginger

¼ teaspoon cloves

Mix well until smooth. Pour into unbaked pie shell. Bake at 450 degrees for 10 minutes. Reduce heat to 350° and bake 40 minutes longer, or until knife inserted into center comes out clean.

CHAPTER THREE

Negotiating the Minefields

There are days when our children are complete angels in public. And then there are the days where we find ourselves trying in vain to negotiate with a very little terrorist while strangers make loud and pointed comments regarding the "poor quality of parenting one sees today," or my personal favorite: "I *never* would have tolerated that sort of behavior from my child." In fact, grocery shopping with a child on the spectrum is a lot like grocery shopping in a field of live landmines. And it can be very difficult to tell what kind of day it's going to be until you're already in the middle of the minefield.

The good news is, we can build up our "mom arsenal" with tools that can help make negotiating the landmines a smoother process. Some of the tools in this chapter are for general use and others more specific to certain adventures.

Basic Training

Reconnaissance is the key

A little preparation can mean the difference between a seamless outing and a disaster. Scope out your destination in advance and if you can't visit, call and ask for the rundown. Long lines? Overhead loudspeakers? Elevators? Escalators? Sliding doors? This will help you decide if you even want to attempt it. Always call ahead before visiting your favorite child-friendly destinations (i.e., museums, zoos). If they have 200 third graders on the schedule for that day, you may want to find an alternative entertainment.

Share the agenda

Our kids don't usually love surprises. Let them know what your plans are in advance, even if they're nonverbal or you aren't sure of their comprehension level. A visual schedule may be helpful here. Speech therapists use these a lot, and you can either buy them online (many of these have odd stick figures that I was entirely unable to decipher) or make your own. I simply took a 3" x 11" piece of card stock, ran a fat piece of velcro down the center, and then kept my digital camera with me for a week and took a picture of everywhere we regularly go—the outside of the bank, post office, grocery store, grandma's house, etc. I printed the photos, trimmed them to size, and put a piece of velcro on the back. (I also found that laminating helps them last longer). I found a sturdy envelope and wrote ALL DONE on the front. Then when we'd go out I could put our destinations on his visual schedule in order. When we had completed an errand we'd take the photo off and put it the envelope.

Deviating from the plan

If you need to stop somewhere unexpectedly and you don't have a photo, there are two things that may be helpful. First, determine if it's really *worth it* to you to stop. In other words, take stock of how the day is going generally, and decide if you're feeling lucky. Second, talk to your child, explain *where* you are going, and why it's important to you ("Mommy needs to buy some stamps.") and what it will be like inside.

Leave early

Oh, stop laughing... it really is possible. Leaving 10 minutes before you actually need to can really take the pressure off, and I find that my son is far calmer and more cooperative if he isn't feeding off of my stress.

Make a fashion statement

Despite your feelings about labeling people, do your child a favor and get them a t-shirt or large button that says, "Got Autism?" or "I'm not trying to misbehave, I'm on the autism spectrum," and keep it in your car or purse. It gives our little guys some breathing room. This is not to imply that we don't have certain expectations about their behavior in public, but if they go into sensory overload and melt down, it will help the people around us to understand and be more tolerant. I for one would rather have people know that he is a child with ASD than have them simply assume he's a spoiled brat. They may think twice before reprimanding the next mom they see in the same situation.

The Good Boy/Girl Lollipop (This is an important one)

Everyone knows the dilemma—our child is acting up and we really need to keep him/her quiet for just a few more minutes. We think to ourselves, "this isn't how it's supposed to work; if my puppy chews up my shoes, I don't give him a biscuit," but we are *desperate*, so we reluctantly give them a special treat to keep the peace even though we know we are reinforcing behavior we probably shouldn't.

I got sick of this situation sneaking up on me so I decided to head it off. I call it the "Good Boy Lollipop" and it has literally changed our lives. Now when we arrive somewhere and I see little signs of restlessness, I pull a lollipop out of my purse like a magician pulling a rabbit out of a hat, hold it up, and ask, "Do you know what this is?" (That always gets a smile.) "This is a Good Boy Lollipop. To get this lollipop I need you to be as good a boy as you can. Can you do that for Mommy?" (Again a big smile.) Then, with great ceremony, I present him with his Good Boy Lollipop. He is thrilled by getting a lollipop *and* having the chance to show what a good boy he can be (the lollipop also gives him some positive sensory input he can focus on) and I am not having to give a treat to an out-of-control kid. Everyone wins. (Remember this only works if it is a *special* treat—lollipops are never given as a "regular" snack.)

Note: There are tons of all natural lollipops with no artificial colors or flavors available. We like Yummy Earth® and Trader Joe's®, but there are many different brands available in stores and online. Giving your poor kid a dose of red dye #3 to try and help him behave better is *biochemical sabotage*, plain and simple.

Handicap hang tag

If you go to the DMV website for your state you will find a form for a handicap hang tag (hang tags may be a better choice than license plates because it can go with your child). There is a check box for Autism on the form. You simply fill it out, have your doctor sign it, and the DMV mails your child his or her tag. Very often we don't need to use it but it can be a lifesaver on the "tough days."

Get a small backpack (for yourself)

You need a backpack just large enough to hold your purse and a few toys and treats for your child. When you get out of the car, toss your purse and a few odds and ends into it and go. **Do Not Skip This One**. The reason is simple— sooner or later your child will throw a full-blown tantrum or suffer a major meltdown. While you are trying to get a screaming, flailing child off of the floor, you will lean down and one (or both) of the following will happen: your shoulder bag will swing down and bonk your already-hysterical child on the head, or the entire contents of your purse will go skidding across the floor. Setting your purse on the ground before attempting to wrestle the aforementioned kid won't help. Upon hoisting said kid into your arms you now are faced with having to do a squat that would impress Arnold Schwartzenegger in order to retrieve your purse.

Ask for and accept help (tough but important)

There are angels of mercy all around us if we learn to ask for and accept help.

In the wild days prior to the addition of spironolactone to reduce abnormally high testosterone levels, tantrums were a major problem for us, both home and away. One day we went to Tractor Supply, a farm supply store close to home. Within moments of entering the store (OK, I had *not* put him in a cart—Parenting Mistake #198), he went ballistic—stark raving, screaming, flailing, kicking, head-bangingly ballistic. I had to essentially pin him to the floor to keep him from injuring himself or other store patrons while

I tried to "talk him down." As you can imagine, we attracted a small crowd, with people staring in horror as my son and I wrestled on the floor. At that moment, a clerk walked over and asked if I had a list. Barely looking up, I handed him the list I'd brought. While I worked at controlling my son, he went through the store and retrieved all of the items in record time, swiped the credit card I dug out of my bag for him, and proceeded to wheel the cart outside. I carried my raging son out of the store and wedged him into his car seat as this wonderful man piled my purchases in the back. With my son finally strapped in, and on the verge of tears myself, I turned around to thank this kind soul. He smiled and said, "You did a great job in there. My autistic son is 11 now. It will get better. Just have faith."

Car sanity

For those with sensory integration difficulties an automobile can be a stressful place. If you think about it cars produce an impressive number of obnoxious sounds. For most of us they are a mild annoyance, but they have the ability to send our kids reeling. I have found that it is far easier to *prevent* sensory overload than to pull my son out of it, sensory overload being not unlike quicksand in this regard. Here are some really simple things that we can do to ensure that riding in the car is a positive experience:

- ◆ Close the door and put on all seatbelts *before* putting the key in the ignition. (Ding, ding, ding…)
- ◆ Leave the radio off for the first 5 minutes of the trip. Then if you want to listen to the radio, find something soothing. You may want to sit in your back seat and test

the volume. I was amazed at how loud the radio was in the back of my car.

◆ Make a family rule that the radio must be turned *off* before you get out of the car. No one likes getting blasted by the radio when they turn on the engine, especially kids with sensory issues.

◆ If you have GPS, keep the volume at a level where you can hear clearly but it's not too loud for your child. GPS voices can be annoying.

◆ If the radio station you're listening to starts to go to static, simply turn it off ASAP rather than trying to find better reception with the "seek" button, which can produce unpleasant surprises.

◆ Try not to accidentally leave your turn signals on while driving down the highway.

◆ Keep the temperature moderate.

◆ Open windows with wind rushing around may be too much sensory input. Watch for the signs of overload.

◆ Try not to run wipers over a relatively dry windshield—use an intermediate setting to prevent screeching.

◆ Turn off the headlights before taking the keys out of the ignition. When it comes to dinging, less is always better.

Supply list

You might look as though you're packing for safari, but the following items are worth taking along. You can neatly contain pretty much all necessary supplies with a plastic tote that fits on the seat or floor next to your child and another one for the floor on the front passenger seat. Keeping things in totes will make them easier to find in emergency situations, and it will keep the interior of your car neater, thereby helping to prevent visual sensory overload.

Kid's bin (back seat)

◆ Handful of small toys that are "special car toys"

◆ Two or three small "special car books"

◆ **Sunglasses.** Let your child pick them out—they seem to know instinctively what level of blockage they are most comfortable with. (And you probably want to go with adult glasses. Kids' sunglasses get recalled for lead paint way too often.) My son *loves* his sunglasses, and wears them whenever we go anywhere. Besides making him look cool, they soften the edges of the world around them both indoors and out, and allow kids to get through florescent-lit superstores with less discomfort.

◆ Child-sized earplugs for emergencies

◆ Lunch box with snacks—let your child pick this out too.

◆ Small thermos of water (stainless steel is better than plastic)

◆ Headphones and CD player if your child likes to listen to Auditory Integration CDs in the car.

◆ Stories on tape/CD (check your local library) A.A. Milne's *Winnie the Pooh* and *The Wind in the Willows* were favorites. There are lots more choices for older kids.

◆ An extra set of clothes. (You just never know.)

◆ Diapers, pull ups, and wipes if needed

Mom's Bin (front seat)

◆ Stash of Good Boy/Girl Lollipops (well-hidden)

◆ Stimming toy (Koosh, Spaghetti Ball, towel, or whatever

works best to soothe your child) to be brought out in case of emergency

◆ Sunglasses for mom. When I put mine on, I remind my son to put on his. Big dark sunglasses are a great help in a crisis—even the coolest and most levelheaded moms have been known to shed a few tears during an ASD tantrum.

◆ MP3 player & headphones

◆ Set of earplugs for you

◆ Rescue Remedy®, if it helps either of you—a lot of moms swear by it.

◆ A can of nuts and a few granola bars for mom

◆ Digestive enzymes in a small pill box, in case you end up stuck somewhere where GFCF is not available, or if you find out that they accidentally ate something containing gluten or casein. For Fiengold kids, caffeine can often calm them down if they've accidentally eaten something loaded with phenols. Coca-Cola Classic® is probably the best here, although black coffee (sugar, no milk) also works well. Coke's formula predates artificial flavors and colors, and has not changed in a hundred years. Mountain Dew®, on the other hand, is full of yellow dye as well as caffeine and won't have the same effect.

◆ Recent photo of your child in case they get lost. No one likes to think about the possibility, but this is *imperative* for our nonverbal kids. (For the same reason, it's a good idea to keep an ID bracelet on nonverbal kids, including name and phone number.)

◆ Copy of Supplements/Meds list

◆ Midday supplements

- Antibacterial hand wipes—especially if your child is immunosuppressed and catches "bugs" easily. Great for wiping off shopping carts.
- Handicap hangtag if needed.

Trunk
- Folding stroller for emergencies (umbrella style for older kids).
- Roadside emergency kit with first-aid kit
- Travel blanket

Shopping

Shopping is one of the worst minefields for moms of ASD kids, and a good dose of realism helps here. The days of wandering the mall aimlessly and puttering up and down every single isle at the grocery store are simply over for the time being. It is possible to make shopping much easier on yourself, and your child, with a little planning.

Come prepared
As in all grand adventures, Good Boy/Girl Lollipops, water, a snack, a stim toy, and a good sense of humor are imperative for success.

Reconnaissance
Always call in advance to find out the following:
◆ When is their busiest time? (Plan your trip for any other time)
◆ Do they have what you are looking for? (There's nothing worse that getting there only to discover that they don't even *carry* it.)
◆ In what department is it located?
◆ If you only need one or two items, can they put them at the customer service desk for you? (Explain that you have a special needs child and will need assistance. It's better to swallow some pride in advance than to set our kids up for a meltdown).

Avoid superstores if you possibly can
Way too much sensory input! You may save a dollar or two

on toilet paper, but you child will be a wreck. I always ended up spending at least 25% more at superstores anyway. I was far more likely to impulse buy when surrounded with shiny stuff. Much better to choose a small, quiet store that will meet 90% of your shopping needs—the other 10% probably isn't that important anyway and you can always pick it up when you are alone.

Share the agenda
Tell your child where you are going and why. Let them use their visual schedule.

Always have a list written out ahead
Wandering aimlessly is really *not* an option for most of our kids. I base my shopping list on my weekly menu and write it out in order of location. If you always go to produce first, that's where your list should start. Unless you buy exactly the same thing every time and have an extraordinary memory, it is unfair to everyone involved try to shop without a list.

Sunglasses and earplugs
If your child is going through an extremely sensory-overloaded phase allow him/her to wear sunglasses and earplugs in the store. It can help limit the amount of new sensory input that they will be bludgeoned with.

Car to cart (this one is important!)
I always try to park close to a shopping cart return. I snag a cart and bring it back to the car, and then transfer my son directly from the car seat into the cart. *His feet DO NOT*

touch the ground. If it looks as though he's going to balk, the Good Boy Lollipop comes out. It's a cheery distraction that makes the transition easier. If your kid is under 10 you can probably still wedge him in a shopping cart somehow.

Unless your child is very nearly recovered, odds are good that if you let him walk into a store under his own steam you'll never make it past the automatic glass doors or the shiny produce racks. If you finally make it past the blasted doors and then to try to stuff him into a shopping cart, you're facing a Battle Royale and you haven't even gotten out your grocery list yet.

Good Boy/Girl Lollipop

Use it. Stay in tune to your kid's body language. If you sense that things are starting to go downhill, get the lollipop out *before* the bad behavior starts. It can turn things around fast.

Let them choose

I always try to let my son make some choices (usually between two mom-approved items) at the store. It gives him a job and helps build decision-making skills.

Don't dawdle

Shopping is a lot of strain on our kids' sensory systems— florescent lights, loudspeakers, music, checkout scanners, and competing smells can all cause sensory overload. Out of kindness to my son, I try to come prepared and get in and out of the store as fast as I can. I also make an effort to stay away from the seafood counter and detergent isle if at all possible. If my son starts to go into overload, I get out his spaghetti ball (stim toy) so he can self soothe, and I go into high-speed mode. So what if I look like a refugee from the old Supermarket Sweepstakes?

Checkout

I always try to have my grocery store card, coupons, and bank card ready as I get up to the checkout line. If the line gets "stuck," or the sound of scanning is making him crazy, swallow some more pride and explain to the checker that you have "a special needs child who is about to come unglued" and could someone in customer service please check you out so you can get him out of there before the explosion.

End on a high note

I always try to end even the craziest trip on a high note. I thank my son for being a good boy and helping mom do the shopping, and I remind him of what good grocery choices he made "all by himself." If he was wild, I ask him to try not to do whatever it was the next time because "it makes people sad." (Child psychologists, please don't bother fussing—it's something he understands and it works for us). Even if it was a tough trip, I always mention something he did well. Consistently ending on a high note (no matter what) helps him to remember it as a positive experience, and has made each subsequent trip easier.

Eating Out

Sometimes you simply have to take a child with ASD into a restaurant. (Often this involves out-of-town doctor's appointments.) A sense of humor, positive attitude and realistic expectations are imperative for this operation.

Choose wisely

Make sure the restaurant you choose has food your child can and will eat. Family-style restaurants are the *only* type worth considering at this junction. We avoid high-end "water goblet" restaurants like the plague—they are generally not set up for children of any sort, much less our sometimes-unpredictable ones. (**Note:** You can find a list of "ASD Mom-Approved" restaurants in the resources chapter.)

Atmosphere

Call or visit restaurants in advance. Is it a quiet place with low-key décor and booths, or is it bustling, with stuff hanging all over the walls, loud music, and an open kitchen? If you can't hear the host over the music when you call, you pretty much have your answer.

Know the menu

If your child is on a special diet you'll need to see the menu in advance. Most places keep their menu online—if not, call during a slow time and talk to the manager. A good restaurant manager knows every ingredient and will be glad to help you out. It's also a good idea to keep some dietary enzymes with you just in case.

Order in advance

If you have to eat at a busy time for the restaurant and waiting is not your child's strong suit, call in your order in advance for "dine in." Most restaurants will do this if you explain that you have a special needs child who when hungry or stuck waiting too long is capable of single-handedly emptying a restaurant… a little humor goes a long way here.

Make a fashion statement

Bring your ASD shirt or pin along just in case.

Carry them in

Until my son's transition issues were resolved I would carry him into restaurants and put him down when we arrived at our booth. The alternative was often to have him walk in and get "stuck" on something, making transitioning to the table nearly impossible.

Booths

Booths ROCK. If your kid is too big for a high chair but needs containment, a booster seat in a booth is perfect. Your kid sits on the inside and adult sits on the outside. If possible pull the table toward you a bit and you'll have a perfect fit.

Recruit the staff… don't be shy

Hosts: I always ask the hosts if they can try to find us a booth in a relatively quiet area. (Sometimes nearby tables full of chattering kids make my son sad).

Wait staff: Introduce yourself and your kids and (remember your sense of humor!) let them know that you may need a little extra help, but assure them that you also tip well.

Bring entertainment

In addition to the official restaurant crayons, we always bring a few small toys—doled out one at a time. A Good Boy/Girl Lollipop can help refocus their attention and isn't substantial enough to make much of a dent in their appetite.

Be willing to leave

I have had to set some boundaries for my son so he learns that some behavior is simply not acceptable. If he is acting up beyond what I consider regular bored-kid behavior and has chosen to ignore my warnings, I will call over the waitperson, ask that our meals be packaged to go, and we leave. It's actually very easy. I explain why we are leaving and that we can try again next week. After doing it once or twice, he realized that it was no idle threat and is usually on his best behavior in restaurants.

Be kind to the kitchen

Unless it is still moving or actively on fire, I don't send food back. It confuses my son (should he eat or not eat?) and annoys the staff.

Pay when your food arrives

For nearly a year I paid my bill and asked for to-go containers when our food arrived. The waitperson is always willing to do this and it avoids confusion should you have to leave under less-than-perfect circumstances.

Tidy up

I always try to keep the table neat and not trash the area. It's nice when the staff at a restaurant is glad to see our kids again.

Tip well

We ask an awful lot from our wait staff and they usually go above and beyond the call of duty for our families. It's nice when they remember our kids and are glad to see them again.

Call the manager

If your waitperson was really great—like if your kid had a tantrum and they bagged your food, settled the check, and held your screaming kid while you collected toys, or if they kept your preschooler giggling nonstop with a litany of knock-knock jokes—take the time to call the manager and tell them. People complain all the time, but rarely do they remember to compliment the staff for a job well done. Warning: It becomes a habit.

Socializing

The Military has Spec Ops (Special Operations) and we have Soc Ops (you guessed it, Social Operations). Play dates and socializing can be difficult for our kids and hard on us too. It's not easy to avoid making comparisons and sometimes we can't help but feel sad that our little guys don't have the same skill sets as their peers yet. The key word here is *yet*. I always try to remember how much progress my son has made. If I need to see it in black and white, I have his daily report to put things into perspective for me. If I feel the need to compare today against anything, I compare it to the day we started my son's recovery. To steal an old line: "We've come a long way, baby."

ASD vs. neurotypical friends

Everyone has their own feelings about this. Some moms I know prefer for their children to socialize predominantly with other children with ASD, some feel neurotypical (NT) kids are a better choice. Originally my son found some of the behaviors of other children with ASD very scary and preferred the company of neurotypical kids. Later, neurotypical children talking when he was nonverbal made him cry. Rather than carve anything in stone one way or the other, I try to read my son's signals and remain flexible.

Have food, will travel

My son brings his lunchbox everywhere. He loves it. He picked it out himself and it is always packed with food he likes and recognizes. If he wants to try something new while he is socializing, that's great, but he doesn't have to run the risk of getting overly hungry (never a good place for him).

Let them choose

Don't force your kids to spend time with children they can't stand, even if their mother is a good friend. My son has very good instincts and if he doesn't like someone, I have to trust him. There may be an underlying sensory reason, or the kid may just be a jerk. Developing social skills is tough enough; trying to "desensitize" a child to someone with whom they aren't comfortable just makes it tougher. Heck, I know people I'd rather not be around—I don't force myself to spend time with them in hopes of "getting over it."

Give other kids a heads-up

I explain to other children that my son can't talk right now but that he can understand what they say. It helps clear things up *before* there is confusion or feelings get hurt. Kids are, on average, very understanding and accepting if given the facts.

Share the agenda

Before every social situation, I let my son know where we are going, who will be there, what we will be doing and why. That way there are no surprises.

The host with the most

Before children come to our house I talk to my son about being "a good host" and what that entails—sharing, showing someone around, and playing together. Most kids with

ASD are very bright, and it does them no favors to assume they cannot learn basic manners.

Patience pays off

Be patient—getting past "parallel play" can take longer for our kids. But once they do engage with other children, the rewards are that much sweeter for them. Have faith that it will come in its own time. (In the meantime, it's good to remember that parallel play is perfectly OK with most kids, even neurotypical ones.)

Staying on the bench

Allowing kids to be kids is tough work for a mom, and especially tough for moms of ASD kids. I would dearly love to be at my son's side to soften every situation, but he'd never learn that way. I try to let him be his own little person and step in only when I see rudeness or unkindness. (Intentional or otherwise, we have an obligation to nip that in the bud.) Difficult as it is to reprimand our own children for rudeness, if we don't teach them what's appropriate socially they will forever struggle to make, and more importantly *keep*, friends.

Butterfly and wallflower

My son has gone through social periods and shy periods. I've found it's better to just let him go through each phase in his own time and consider it part of the growth process.

Keep the faith

I have to be very careful not to get discouraged around neurotypical kids my son's age. I try to remember that he is simply on a different journey and that there is a plan for him.

Preschool, Daycare, and Schools

I'll start by saying that if you have been asked to remove your child from a school, preschool, or daycare center, *you are not alone.* Most of the moms I know have had their child ousted from at least one "open-minded, nurturing educational environment." Don't take it personally—most places don't have the staff or the skill sets to work constructively with kids like ours. It doesn't mean we won't *ever* find a good fit, it simply means we're not there quite yet.

(On the other hand, if you've found a place where your child is thriving, stick with it! They are hard to come by.)

We are very lucky to have an exemplary special needs system in our district. Despite being severely overburdened (and under-funded) the teachers and administrators are able to ensure that kids receive the services they need. Unfortunately, this is not always the case. Many public school systems are simply overwhelmed by the sheer number of children needing services and they are striving to do the best they can with limited resources. There are many books that can help you learn what your options are within the public school system (see Pre-screened Resources). It is definitely worth doing your homework. In the case of private schools and daycares, there is often a learning curve regarding ASD, but if they are willing to work with you, all the better.

ASD experience

Find out if the school has any prior experience in educating children with ASD. They may have special requirements (such as a shadow or half days) until the teacher is comfortable with our child's skill set.

Meet the teachers in advance

Take the time to meet the teachers and aides with your child. If your child loathes him or her on site, or if you feel the teacher isn't a good fit for some reason (lack of sense of humor comes directly to mind) you may want to see if there is a spot in a different class available or keep shopping around.

Visit classrooms

Check out the prospective classroom. Is it barely controlled chaos? What is your first impression—relatively quiet and well-organized, or noisy, chaotic, and visually overwhelming? Try to see the room through your child's eyes. An out of control classroom should be a deal breaker.

Go to school with them

Arrange it so that you can go to class with your child for the first day or two. Despite the school's protestations, I can assure you that having one adult sitting silently in the back of a classroom will *not* irreparably disrupt the flow of learning.

Shadow

If needed, ensure that your child has a shadow (an adult who assists them) in the classroom.

Get on schedule

Get a copy of the classroom schedule and begin practicing it at home well *before* the start of school.

Daily reports

Purchase a small notebook and ask (or insist if it comes to that) that your child's teacher provide a daily report for the first few weeks. Ensure them that one or two lines is sufficient—we are not asking for *War and Peace* here.

Set some hard and fast rules

Discuss with the teacher what you consider to be unacceptable (It may be no throwing toys, chewing of clothes, or pushing of other kids) and make sure that they understand that you wish to be contacted should any of these things occur.

Make it *crystal clear* that self-injury (head-banging, biting or scratching of oneself, etc.) is not acceptable and that you expect the staff to take immediate action to protect your child from hurting himself further and notify you ASAP.

Meals

Let your child pack snacks and his or her own lunch (with mom oversight of course.) They love knowing what's waiting for them. Our kids tend to be picky eaters and many are on special diets. Odds are good that school food is not going to be on their agenda.

Expectations

Set healthy expectations. We know better than anyone that transitions can be tough for our kids. It may take a few weeks for them to acclimate to a school environment.

It's not a race

Education is a meandering path, not a destination. We live in a naturally competitive society and it can be difficult not to compare our child to his or her peers. Try to remember that, like everyone else, our kids will excel in some things and struggle with others. There is no finish line so let them enjoy the journey at their own pace.

Doctor Visits

Children with ASD spend an inordinate amount of time in doctor's offices, and advance planning can make the difference between success and *total disaster*, which is exhausting for both parent and child. Here are a few ideas that can make it easier for everyone, including the medical staff.

The right doctor
If your current doctor does not believe that your child can and will recover (even though he or she may not know how to make that happen right now), *find a new doctor*. As Autism Moms, we have very limited time and financial resources. We do not need to expend either one on someone who believes recovery for our children is hopeless.

D.A.N. doctors
If you are not already working with a D.A.N.! (Defeat Autism Now!) doctor, you may want to try and get on the schedule of one in your area. These are the only real "autism experts" in the medical community. No matter what you may have heard or read, D.A.N.! doctors are not "quacks," they are simply regular MDs with an interest in treating autism as a *medical* rather than a psychological condition, often because they have a child with autism themselves. (A geographic list of D.A.N.! doctors can be found on many autism support websites.) **Note:** Even if you see a D.A.N.! doctor, you will want to keep an open-minded primary care doctor in your own city for usual day-to-day "kid stuff." Even if they are nearby (which they often are not) D.A.N.! docs are usually

extremely busy and odds are there's a fairly long waiting time for an appointment.

Get the most bang for your buck

As the insurance industry is still hiding behind the "autism is a psychological condition" curtain, you will find that most of your child's treatment is paid out of pocket. This means we have to shop around; find out what the doctor's rates are, what do the labs charge for tests, do we get the insurance company's negotiated rate? We have to put our resources where they will do the most good. Its not impolite, its just good business.

Be smart about supplements

If your doctor's recommended supplements are out of your budget, just come out and *tell* them! Your doctor will gladly help you work out alternatives. Ask for the name of the supplement and the recommended dosage and look elsewhere. www.vitacost.com has some great inexpensive supplements, and Amazon carries a incredible number of supplements at discounted prices. I can assure you that your doctor is more concerned with getting the supplements into your kid than the specific brand you use.

Timing can impact success

When scheduling an appointment, try to pick the time that is best for your child. My son is a morning kind of guy (Heaven help me) and is usually most cooperative then, so we usually try for morning appointments whenever possible.

Prep for meetings

I always fax or email a list of questions or topics I want to discuss with my doctor a few days in advance of our meeting and then bring a copy to the appointment so I can write down the answers. This is a great way to ensure that everyone is on the same page and I don't have to count on my memory alone.

Feed the troops prior to maneuvers

Unless your child is fasting for a specific test, feed everyone (yourself included) before going to the doctor's office. I usually bring snacks and Good Boy Lollipops along just in case. A hungry child is usually a cranky child.

Brief the troops

I always let my son know where we are going and what the doctor will be doing at the appointment. That way there will be no unpleasant surprises.

Get to know the nurses

Remember to ask the nurses how *they* are doing. They have a very tough job, give it everything they've got, and certainly deserve our respect and kindness. The nurses I've met know more about ASD than most people could put together in a lifetime. They have a wealth of knowledge that few people tap. Most are more than willing to answer your questions and can tell you beautiful stories of recovery. Who knows, it might be just what you needed to hear that day!

Copay

It's a simple trick really, but I always write out my check and pay the copay (or whole bill if necessary) *while we are still in the waiting room.* By the time the appointment is over, my son is ready to go, and we've usually tapped the last of his patience. It's hard to pay a bill while someone is trying to literally drag you out the door.

Entertaining the troops

If you need to have a in-depth discussion with your doctor, you may want to schedule a conference call. If a conference call isn't convenient, we bring a portable DVD player and headphones to the appointment—that way my son can watch his favorite movie and I can have an uninterrupted conversation regarding his recovery.

Background materials

Bring your 3-ring binder with your test results, doctors notes, etc. (see Chapter 1) for reference.

Have faith

Above all, trust your instincts and keep an open mind. Kids with ASD can and do recover. If you need to reassure yourself, google "autism recovery stories" and watch the videos or read the stories.

The Family Vacation

When you've got a kid on the autism spectrum, vacations are often the Great Unknown. They can be a grand adventure or a total disaster; very often it's *our* attitude that is the deciding factor.

Traveling with a child with ASD takes a wicked sense of humor, a lot of patience, and the ability to haul enough provisions to stage an invasion of a third world country. (I'm pretty sure Pack Mule is in our job description somewhere).

Pike's Peak or bust

Choose your destination wisely. It is important to be very realistic about your child's capability to handle a change of venue. Transportation options will play a huge role in your decision. Where we *want* to go and where we *can* go may be two very different places for a while. Fear not, someday our children will be ready for all of the exotic locales we've been dreaming of... we are just not there quite yet.

Planes

Do the words "sensory nightmare" mean anything to you? Airplanes are the pinnacle of *confined sensory overload*. Here's the short version: beeping wands and x-ray machines, smooshed seating, blowing fans, hot on the tarmac, cold in the air, roaring engines, crying baby, too many people with too much cologne, popping ears, way high up, turbulence, stinky food, and rattling carts. That about covers it.

Only if it is the *only option* available to you do you want to subject a child with ASD to air travel. More often than not it's tough on them, tough on you, and often tough on everyone else on the plane. There are no doubt exceptions to this, but I have honestly only met one kid with ASD who thought flying was fun and he is very close to recovered.

Booking flights

Tell your travel agent (or if booking online include in the "special requests" section) that you will be traveling with a special needs child and will need extra assistance throughout. You may want to bring this to the attention of the airline representative behind the desk at the airport as well. Try to get a golf cart to the security area, and then to your gate. There is an awful lot of sensory candy to be seen walking through the airport and it can make getting to your gate on time very difficult.

Security

We can't talk about planes without touching on airport security. If you use liquid supplements you will have to check them (you may want to say a little prayer as you watch them roll away to the baggage area). Grab the first non-grouchy-appearing person you can find, explain that you are traveling with a special needs child and will need help (actually *lots* of help). Sometimes watching the bags get x-rayed keeps them entertained for a bit, but usually the buzzing, beeping, and waiting is a little much. Headphones or earplugs may be helpful.

I should also mention that for reasons unknown, every single time my poor son has had to fly he ends up being randomly selected for a full luggage search and wand scan. Talk about adventure!

Trains

We *love* the train. Trains are a great alternative to planes for kids with ASD, and Amtrak® serves all the major cities. It's admittedly slower than air travel but far less stressful and besides, 99% of our kids *adore* trains for some strange reason. (If there's a boy on the spectrum who doesn't have a train set of his own I haven't run into him yet.) Train stations are usually a lot less stressful than airports; you can haul everything you need right on board with you and check your larger items.

While riding the rails kids can wander around, go to the dining car or the snack car (less formal and a better choice usually), and many trains have a very cool observation car that is virtually all glass. The coach seats (only two to a side) are large, really do recline, and there's ample room to spread out with blankets and toys. If you put your child in the window seat, which is endlessly entertaining for most kids, and take the aisle seat for yourself, you can create a little "room" of your own. (Springing for your own private room is also an option most planes don't offer, and in some cases it may be well-worth the price.) The train has a very soothing rhythm that helps little guys fall sleep. My son has an absolute *blast* traveling by train. The only problem we've ever run into is that he's reluctant to get off! It may be slower than air travel, but it's a far more peaceful environment. Night trains are also worth considering—you can feed them in Richmond, tuck them in for the night, and wake up in sunny Florida the next morning… no driving required!

Automobiles

Cars are the mode of transportation our kid know best and may be most comfortable with on longer journeys. They are, however, totally limiting as far as moving around, and your kids will need frequent stops to stretch their legs and take bathroom breaks. Traveling by car also allows you a tremendous amount to freedom—if you need to stop, you simply pullover and get a room somewhere. However, gas prices, vehicle reliability, and parental exhaustion must all be taken into consideration before embarking on a major road trip. Personally, I'd check the Amtrak schedule before considering it.

Regardless of your destination or mode of conveyance, here are some tips that may help you and your family on your adventures:

Share the agenda

A few weeks in advance of your trip, tell your child *where* you are going, *why* you are going, and *how* you will get there, including each step of the journey. If you're taking a train, then getting a rental car and driving for a half hour, make that clear. Kids on the spectrum are pretty literal and failing to prepare them for each separate leg of the journey can result in a meltdown when you least need it. Using photos may help this process—you can lay out each step visually as you explain the trip.

Chatting about the trip repeatedly (and cheerfully!) ahead of time will make it easier for your child to transition.

Contact your doctor

A week or two prior to your trip, you will want to stock up on medications and supplements. It might be wise to ask your doctor to prescribe a mild liquid sedative for your child in case of emergency.

Organize your itinerary

Get a report folder (the kind with the 3 prongs and 2 pockets) 3-hole punch and consolidate your travel materials. I put them in order of need. Itinerary, train ticket, rental car, hotel etc. A few post-it file tabs make it very easy to locate things with one hand. The pockets are great for tucking maps and receipts.

Rental house vs. hotel

Rental houses have a lot of advantages over hotels when traveling with a child with ASD, and they are generally less expensive than hotels. Having a kitchen is always a cost-saver when traveling with kids, and a real *lifesaver* if your child is on a GF/CF diet. A rental house also tends to feel a little more "homelike," which makes it easier to stay on a schedule (albeit a more fluid one) while traveling. A fenced yard (and maybe a pool, depending on your child's reliability level) can be worth its weight in gold. *And* you don't have to worry about getting complaints from the occupants of the room next door if things get a little loud!

Several websites (www.VRBO.com is one) maintain an extensive list of vacation rentals from coast to coast, with photos and amenities for each one. It's well-worth checking out when planning a vacation.

Hotels generally work OK for a night or two. When making reservations you need to make sure that the room has a refrigerator, and inform the staff *in advance* that you will be traveling with a special needs child. I always ask for a room in a quiet area of the hotel on the first floor, especially if oceanside balconies happen to be the hotel's claim to fame. Once you check in, let the staff know that you have a child with autism and you may need some assistance now and again. (As autism rates continue to rise, I've found more and more hotel staff seem to have first-hand experience with exactly what that means and a response like, "I understand—my sister's boy is autistic, too," is getting a lot more common than it was a few years back.)

Rental cars

Rental cars are a great convenience and can be easy to transition to with a little preparation. Try to get an idea of what car they will assign you and print a black and white photograph of the car to give to your child. That way you can all guess what color the car will be when you pick it up! I discuss with my son that it may look, smell, and maybe *sound* a little different than our car, but that it will be fun to discover all of the different things about it. I know too many moms who forgot this step and as a result couldn't get their kid into the rental car for love or money. (Remember, preparing a child with ASD *ahead of time* for new experiences will go a long way toward preventing major transition problems.)

Coolers

Most of us travel with a cooler for supplements, medications, and snacks. For road trips, the big plastic ones are great, but I've found the soft-sided ones are easier to use if you're using public transportation. They allow you the flexibility to strap it to the handles of a rolling suitcase or throw it over your shoulder. If you plan on checking it into airline luggage you may want to wrap the contents in bubble wrap.

Gainful employment

Give your kid (or each kid if you have several) a job. Any job will do, but make sure it's something they can focus on while bored. Counting birds on telephone wires, or the number of red cars on the road works, if you can't think of anything else. Have fun with it.

Supply List

◆ Supplement/medicine list
◆ Recent photo of your child
◆ Lightweight umbrella stroller (even if they're pretty much past the stroller stage, it might be the only way to get them from point A to point B in a crisis)
◆ ASD T-shirt
◆ DVD Player, headphones and a handful of favorite videos (well worth every penny of the $100 or so you pay for it) A must for air travel.
◆ Sunglasses and ear plugs
◆ MP3 player for you
◆ Dietary enzymes (just in case)

- Toys and book (stim toy is imperative)
- Snacks and drinks (no artificial colors—period. You do not want to be trapped in a small space with a child having a phenol reaction, trust me)
- Good Boy/Girl Lollipops
- Backpack
- ID bracelet for your child

Go back to square one

If things go haywire, simply calm everyone down as quickly as possible (you and Dad too!) and start your day over. Be sure and tell your kids that you are starting the day over, and be cheerfully determined when you do it, even if you're not *feeling* particularly cheery. You can even go have breakfast again (that cracks my son up). Do *not* let one negative experience taint the remainder of the trip. Remember the National Lampoon *Vacation* movies… was it as bad as *that*? Probably not. Let it go, start over, and have a blast.

Amusement Parks

Personally, if I owned both an amusement park and hell, I'd happily rent out the amusement park and live in hell. That said, when there are husbands, siblings, and extended family involved, eventually amusement parks will make their way into your life. Look at it this way—it's a great way to assess how well your kid's recovery is going. Here are some tips for making it through in one piece.

Reconnaissance

Go to the park's website in advance. Print out a map. Figure out where the food, the age-appropriate rides, and some quiet family areas (hey its worth a shot) are located.

Start small

If possible start small. County fairs are an easy way to begin. If they are not an option, try to find a park that is well laid out and has some natural green space (Busch Gardens®, Sea World®, etc.). You may also want to start with a one-day event; you don't want to discover that amusement parks make your child crazy after you've arrived for a five-day stay at Disney World®.

If Disney World is the destination, seriously consider renting a beach house on the Atlantic coast, and day-tripping it (it's less than an hour from Cocoa Beach, and a little more than an hour from the quieter Ormond Beach, where you can rent a beach bungalow with a fully fenced yard for around $600 a week) rather than staying on-site. That way, if the sensory extravaganza that is Disney World is simply not bearable for your child (it happens), your family's vacation won't be a total bust. Playing in the white sand of Ormond's uncrowded beaches might be more to your child's liking, and the city actually boasts an official "autism-friendly" playground! The rest of the family can day-trip it to Disney and Sea World, and everyone can meet up at the bungalow at the end of each day, tired and happy.

Do your homework

No matter what your intended destination, spend a few minutes online and find something in the same community that you can do with your child in case you need to leave abruptly (a park, a quiet wildlife refuge, or even the pool at the hotel).

Prepare the troops

Make sure everyone (yourself included) gets a good night's sleep the night before. Ensure that everyone eats a protein-filled breakfast that morning to prevent dropping blood sugar and the crankiness that usually accompanies it.

Bring a stroller

All kids get exhausted at amusement parks, many of the larger parks will have strollers available to you if you don't want to carry your own.

Take advantage of available resources

Some larger parks may be able to give your child a handicap pass to help them get through lines, and provide "quiet areas" if you need them. Call in advance to find out how they can help you make this a positive experience for your child.

Plan B

When traveling with more than one child, always have a backup plan (and a backup adult) with you. That way, if the child with ASD needs to leave the amusement park for saner pastures *right now*, you two can leave, and his or her siblings can finish their time at the park. Have a "Plan B" meeting place and time so you can regroup at the end of the day, and use cell phones to keep in touch.

Tantrum Management

No matter how well you plan, tantrums happen. It's important to remember that *all* kids have temper tantrums—they're in no way limited to children with ASD, though our kids have admittedly turned them into a pretty impressive art form! There are tricks to pulling a kid from the depths of a raging tantrum that have been passed down from mom to mom, and they actually do work. What follows is the short course on tantrum management.

If your child is having raging temper tantrums on a regular basis (the kind that include a red face, scowling, punching, and kicking—basically doing a pretty good impression of the Incredible Hulk), you may want to have their testosterone levels checked. A lot of kids on the autism spectrum (both boys *and* girls) have abnormally high testosterone levels, which can lead to uncontrolled rage as well as other more serious health issues including premature puberty. Spironolactone, a relatively old anti-inflammatory drug with a good safety record *and* the side effect of blocking testosterone, can work wonders for kids on the spectrum with high T-levels. Besides causing uncontrollable aggression, testosterone also blocks oxytocin, the "communication and bonding hormone."

Getting abnormal testosterone levels under control can lessen the occurrence of temper tantrums, but they will not completely disappear as long as you're dealing with a small child.

The four steps to tantrum management (and prevention in the future) are a lot like the techniques used by your average bomb-squad: Assess, Extract, Defuse, and Analyze.

Assess the situation

It doesn't take but a second or two for a mom to size up a situation. We're a pretty observant lot. Take a look around. What lit the fuse… sensory overload? Frustration with the child's ability to communicate his desires? Figuring out what caused the tantrum will be imperative in defusing this particular little bomb. You also need to determine whether or not you're dealing with an actual *temper tantrum* or a *meltdown*, and there really is a difference, although most people use the term "tantrum" for both. A meltdown is generally caused by sensory overload, whereas a tantrum usually represents frustration and anger on the child's part. Although the result is similar (an out-of-control kid in a public situation) and they are basically handled in the same way, understanding the difference can go a long way in helping to prevent either one from happening the next time around.

Extract

Get them *out of there* ASAP and lose the audience. Haul your flailing kid off the battlefield. Be willing to leave no matter what. There is no event so important that it's worth subjecting yourself and your child to the scrutiny of those who don't understand, and it's a simple consideration to those around us.

Defuse

Find a quiet place (a bathroom or quiet corner will work in a pinch) and a stim toy and try to talk your child down. Getting upset yourself, or demanding that he stop RIGHT NOW, will simply dump gasoline on the flames. In the first few minutes of a tantrum my son could be pulled out by asking him to calm down, take a deep breath, and help me understand the problem. This will work if you can do it in the first few minutes—after that point they've usually built up a real head of steam and require extraction. Most of our kids respond well to deep pressure (a sensory integration term for bear hug). The bear hug serves two purposes—first, the deep pressure will help them calm down, and second, it prevents self-injury. If your child needs silence, by all means give it to him. My son responded well to quiet soothing discussion. I'd ask him to take some deep breaths, I'd discuss whatever happened to set him off (basically the information you pulled from your original assessment) and then work on integrating some quiet distractions (a favorite stimming toy, a drink of water, or even a question). Every kid responds differently, so see what works best for your child and incorporate that consistently into you "tantrum management system."

Analyze

If you analyze each tantrum after the fact, you can apply the "lessons learned" to your arsenal. Figure out what you learned from this tantrum

What set it off?

How could it be avoided in the future? Often, with non-verbal kids, frustration results when they think we simply don't understand what they want. Explaining firmly but kindly that you *do* understand what he wants, but we can't do that right now (with an explanation of why and perhaps an alternative plan that he can focus on) and following that with a distraction, will often diffuse a temper tantrum *before* it becomes full-blown, as many non-verbal kids have better receptive language than we give them credit for.

What helped him recover the most?

What did you wish you had with you?

CHAPTER FOUR

Friendly Fire

Basic Training

Autism Spectrum disorders can put unintentional strain on our relationships with friends and family. Very often people just don't know what to say, who to believe, or how to help. There are, of course, those outspoken folks with very antiquated ideas about ASD, but as public awareness (and unfortunately incidence) of autism grows, they are thankfully becoming a minority.

Educate

As in most things, true understanding comes from education and experience. A great book for family and friend is Ellen Notbohm's *10 Things Every Child With Autism Wishes You Knew*. It's a quick read and a good guide for helping others get a better understanding of autism. If you don't own it, buy two so you can keep lending one out.

Don't let ASD define your family

That gives autism all the power… after all, how often do you hear people say "we are a cancer family"? We are a family *first* and a family battling autism *second*.

Shift the focus

ASD takes up so very much of our lives that it's easy to get stuck in our own little world. Friends and family can lift us out of that by sharing themselves with us. It's nice to focus on others, hear about their problems (even if they seem like *anthills* compared to ours!) and let their joys and sorrows take the forefront for a while.

Sensor topics

Save conversations about supplements, poop, and I.V. vs. suppository chelation for conversations with those family members who are actively involved in your child's recovery, other Autism Moms, or your doctors. In our excitement over our child's recovery we may run the risk of alienating those we could have educated if we come across as zealots.

Blood Is Thicker than Water, but Not Cod Liver Oil

Dealing with family can be one of the hardest parts of life with a child on the autism spectrum. The following suggestions may seem a little ruthless at first. However, unless you have a lot more free time than the rest of us, there really isn't room in your life for troublemakers, naysayers, and the rest of their ilk, whether they happen to share your DNA or not. The Autism Moms I know have some pretty strong feelings in this arena and have seen and heard it all.

Choose wisely

Always choose your family gatherings wisely. Here are four things to consider before heading out.

1. Are the people attending positive thinkers who make your child feel good about his or herself?

2. Will the venue work for you? (Is the event being held at a city park with no fences? Is the headcount too overwhelming?)

3. What sort of travel will it entail?

4. What kind of day is your child having? (If they're a wreck before 9:00 am, *skip it*. If your child woke up with the stomach flu you wouldn't go… remember that this is a health condition, too. Everyone will understand if you simply say your child isn't feeling well this morning—there's no need to go into gory details.)

Lighten your load

Take a deep breath. Accept that although you may love them dearly, *you cannot change them*, and simply *write off* any family member who falls into the following categories:

- They believe your child is a brat in need of nothing more than a good spanking
- They believe your child is retarded and/or should be institutionalized for the good of everyone in the family.
- They announce that you and your husband should never have had children.
- They believe autism is simply a figment of your imagination, and despite the neurologists' and doctors' reports are convinced that there is nothing really wrong with your child. (I was stunned when I heard a mom tell me about this one)
- They believe you simply need to "toughen up" your child.
- They make *any* cruel, unkind, or derogatory remarks about (or to) your child.

This may seem pretty cold, but we have only so much time and energy, and there is no point wasting either on unkind people, related to you or otherwise. No confrontation is necessary. Just graciously remove your family from their crosshairs. Be unavailable—"very busy that weekend, sorry." Sooner or later they'll quit calling, often a blessing in its own right. Send a Christmas card if you feel guilty. Who knows—perhaps in time the Clue Fairy may visit them and they will feel compelled to adjust their behavior. In the meantime you will have done yourself, and your child, a huge service. Our kids face so many challenges already; insuring that they are surrounded by love and acceptance is *our* responsibility.

Share the journey

Spend time in the company of those family members who love and appreciate your child exactly where he or she is in their journey—people who truly care about their recovery and are supportive of your family's decisions. This allows our kids to experience the joy that comes with having a loving extended family. Remember, "extended family" does not mean you have to share the same DNA. Families are made up of people who care about each other, and are supportive and kind to one another whether they're related by blood or not.

Recruit an older kid to be guide

At family events it's been very helpful to recruit a slightly older cousin or two (girls are usually great at this because they're so naturally nurturing) to help my son socialize. I explain a little about autism and the things he could use help with, and off they go. The support of a slightly older child can be a huge help in paving the way for our kids when it comes to social situations. Every kid on the spectrum should be lucky enough to have cousins like Sofia and Andriana!

Siblings

As the mother of an only child and the sibling of one very cool brother, I am totally unqualified to write this chapter. Thankfully several other moms were gracious enough to share some of their insights.

Relative peace among siblings is necessary for a low stress home. Here are some things that can help make that possible:

Family rules
Everyone has to play by the rules. Some may be adjusted for skill level but the child with ASD doesn't get a "free pass"—it causes resentment among the siblings.

Special time
All kids need individual time, and often the child with ASD seems to get the lion's share. Every week try to arrange for the "neurotypical" children to spend a few hours with one parent doing something they enjoy while their brother or sister does something else.

Daily checkup
Check in with *all* of your kids every single day to see how they are doing—how school is going, and if they have anything special they need to talk about. Some siblings don't feel like "their stuff" is important when compared to autism, and so are hesitant to bring things up on their own.

It's a tough job but somebody's got to do it

Being a sibling to a brother or sister with ASD is not an easy job. They may need a break now and again. A great book for helping siblings deal with autism was actually written by the big sister of a little boy with autism. *All About My Brother* by Sarah Peralta is worth picking up. (It's available at Amazon.)

Born teachers

Very often our children teach each other more than we ever could. Give them space to learn from their siblings, regardless of who is older or younger. They will naturally learn together.

Siblings relations

Your children will establish a relationship that is entirely independent of you and their father. This is natural and should be allowed the space to grow and blossom.

Translators

Very often siblings will "talk" for the child with autism. Decide as a family how much of this is acceptable, and set some ground rules. You may want to talk to your speech therapist to get some ideas.

Same as it ever was

Expect typical sibling rivalry, jealousy, and arguing, even between the child on the spectrum and his "neurotypical" siblings. This is perfectly normal, and probably healthy.

Be honest

Siblings of children with ASD tend to do a lot of worrying. You know all that stuff you worry about—will he ever marry, have kids, go to college? Guess what? Odds are their brother or sister is worrying about the exact same things. It's important to be honest (age-appropriately of course) and try to allay their fears. Don't insult them by telling them they shouldn't worry or nothing's wrong. Kids are naturally intuitive—they know perfectly well that's not the case and will be less likely to approach you next time they have a concern.

Privacy

Teach everyone to respect each other's privacy, and possessions. *All* kids need their own space.

Notes

CHAPTER FIVE

Live Grenades

This chapter touches on four of the touchiest subjects out there. While none of these topics are strictly limited to the autism community, they have serious impact on our lives and the well-being of our kids. They're the topics no one really wants to address, but dealing with them head-on and honestly is critical for Autism Mom survival.

The Caregiver Parent

We are in the delicate position of having to be both parent *and* caregiver to children who are often nonverbal, very literal in their thinking, extremely sensitive to sensory stimulation, and whose comprehension level may yet be unknown. We do this joyfully and without question every single day while we try to maintain the delicate balance required as a "caregiver parent."

Believe in your child's recovery

Believe in your childs' recovery, even (and especially) when no one else does. There are few things in the universe more powerful or that can facilitate greater change than a mother's faith.

My favorite example of this is my great-aunt. Her third daughter was born with severe cerebral palsy back in the 1950s. With a resolve that most of the family and the entire medical community considered merely acute denial (sound familiar?), my great-aunt became a speech, occupational, and physical therapist all rolled into one. She had absolutely no training and little support. Armed with nothing but a mother's faith, she never once doubted that her daughter could and would eventually do things just like everyone else—it would just take more effort. To say that this flew in the face of conventional medicine at the time is an understatement of epic proportions—back then, children with severe CP were wheelchair-bound, had no functional speech and so were considered "retarded," and institutionalization was the recommendation. So my great-aunt simply ignored all the experts. And her daughter did *not* spend her life confined to a wheelchair, nor did she end up in an institution. As a result of her mother's "denial," she learned to both walk and talk. In fact, she grew up to live a full, physically active life, had a successful career in banking, married, and had kids. She was probably the first person to "recover" from cerebral palsy.

Teach them what they need to know

When my mother first told me that story I asked myself, "If my son were to recover tomorrow, have I given him the tools he needs to function in the 4-year-old neurotypical world?" If I was honest with myself, my answer was no. I'd been afraid to allow myself to believe that he could recover. Once he started recovering physically and was able to actually *learn*, I realized we had some serious catching up to do. I now firmly believe that our kids can and *will* recover, even if all the science to make that happen doesn't exist yet for some of them. The question is, when that happens, will we, as parents, have taught them what they need to know?

As parents, it's our job to set and enforce boundaries at home. Sometimes I forget that while he may be on the autism spectrum right now, my son is also a little boy. A little boy who does plain old regular little boy stuff like picking his nose, throwing mud, and leaving clothes strewn around. I try very hard to remember that not every behavioral lapse is autism-related, and that it's my responsibility to help him become a gentleman rather than a hooligan. Our kids deserve to know the basic rules they need to function in the big world out there, and we do them no favors by neglecting to teach them.

Hand over hand

This basically means you gently put your hand over your child's in order to show them how to do something (i.e. his hand over the toothbrush and yours over his showing him how to brush). Therapists use this trick whenever possible, but it really is mom territory. A child who doesn't want a therapist to do hand over hand will often happily let mom show them. It's been a great way to teach my son lots of new life skills. Definitely worth a try!

Give them choices

Whenever possible, let your child make choices—clothes, snacks, whatever. (Giving them a choice between *two things* rather than many makes this easier, by the way.) It gives them a sense of independence, helps with both decision-making skills and communication, and helps assuage the feeling of powerlessness that plagues all children, and non-verbal ones especially. (For this reason, giving children lots of opportunities to make choices can actually reduce the number of temper tantrums in your house.)

Practice makes perfect

Even when it's easier (and faster) for us to just throw on their shoes and socks, or put away their toys ourselves, it's worth the extra time to eventually see that little face glow with the pride of accomplishment from having done it all by themselves. Remember to praise lavishly for all efforts made, even if they haven't quite mastered a task yet. ("Wow, you almost got those shoes on all by yourself!")

Setting expectations

It's important to set reasonable, (age and developmentally appropriate) expectations. This job is obviously easier if you have older kids—you know what three-year-olds *should* be able to do. My son is an only child, so I've had to do a little homework. Luckily, other moms have been more than willing to help me out here. I also started paying closer attention to neurotypical kids my son's age to find out what "age appropriate" behavior actually looks like. (This can be painful, I know, but it really is important.)

I always try to explain the "why" behind my expectations, in terms that my son can easily understand and have meaning to him. ("Because I said so" usually doesn't fly with concrete thinkers like our kids—I just don't think it makes any sense to them). When I asked my son please not to screech (you know that sound!) I explained that it hurts other people's ears, and reminded him of when he had hurting ears; it made perfect sense to him and he really tries to remember not to do it. Our kids are very sensitive and they really can be altruistic if given all the information they need, presented in concrete terms they can understand.

"What we have here is a failure to communicate."

If your child is nonverbal this is a daily event. It's absolutely critical when your non-verbal child is frustrated and whining that you explain that one, you are very sorry but you just do not understand what he/she wants, so he'll have to help you; or two, that you *do* understand, but for whatever reason (and you'd better explain that reason clearly and concretely), the answer for right now is no. Remembering to do this often makes the difference between whining and grumbling, which is usually self-limiting, and a full-blown temper tantrum, which is not.

H.A.L.T.

Hungry. Angry. Lonely. Tired. Recognizing HALT can give you incredible insight into a situation. Our kids do not want to behave badly—there is nearly always a cause for their behavior, and sometimes it's less complicated than we think. If my son seems suddenly close to meltdown, I try to determine first if he's in HALT. Is he hungry? Is he unable to find a favorite horse from his beloved collection? Are his feelings hurt by other kids talking? Is he just tired? Knowing the cause allows us to find the cure.

Speak literally

Our kids are very literal. Odds are good that requests like, "knock it off" or "Give mommy a break," will result in non-compliance simply because the words make *no sense* to them in that context. "Stop jumping on the couch now, please" will generally work better than "Knock it off!" unless you really do want something knocked off, like a lamp, maybe…

and you'll have no one but yourself to blame if that happens.

Keep the volume down

Note: I was lucky to have grown up in a house where people generally did not shout, so remembering not to raise my voice is pretty easy for me. On the other hand, if you grew up in a "yelling household"(much more common in big families with lots of kids), it may take some practice.

Unless your child is about to be hit by a bus, don't shout. It's not particularly effective for altering behavior in children of any stripe, and is guaranteed to send ours into sensory overload, where they'll promptly start stimming and detach even more. They feel bad, we feel bad—it's never worth it in the end. When I feel myself getting frustrated and have the urge to bellow, I know I need a break, even if it's just going in the next room and taking a few deep breaths.

Privacy

Finding a balance between allowing healthy privacy and keeping a child from detaching can be difficult. Kids need alone time as much as we do. Moms are usually adept at telling if our kid is detaching or if they just need time alone. This gets complicated when we second guess ourselves and begin to wonder if we just aren't giving them enough intellectual stimulation. Think back, how much time did your parents spend intellectually stimulating you? Mine let us run and play outside, create adventures, and have imaginary friends. Such was the world before "developmental milestones." My son may have ASD but I also have to remember that he is independent, adventurous, and a little shy. Everyone deserves a little privacy now and then.

Manners

I have said "Please" and "Thank You" a thousand times for my nonverbal son. This may seem silly but when he can finally get his words out, he will know the importance of both. Never discount the importance of teaching manners.

Fake it

I believe in "faking it until you make it." Here's an example: Every single time my son dragged me over and pushed my hand toward the kitchen faucet, I would say, "Go find your glass and bring it to the sink if you're thirsty and you can have a drink." Then I would scan the room and we'd get it together. We did this day in and day out, 900 times at least. I will never forget the beautiful day when I said that for the 901st time and he understood. Truly understood! He looked around, ran and got his glass, brought it to the sink and poured his very own drink of water from the tap for the first time in his life. Now he does it all the time. Don't give up before the miracles happen.

Little Ears

When my mother was growing up, the family matriarchs would sit around and talk. When they would come upon a subject that was not child appropriate someone would pointedly say "Little Ears" and they would continue their conversation in Greek.

There are many days I wish I spoke Greek. Kids probably hear more adult conversations than at any other time in history (an inevitable result of not letting them out of our sight) and frankly I don't think it's a good thing. Our kids probably hear far more than they ever wanted to, and far too often it's about them. This goes double for our nonverbal kids.

Aphasia

D.A.N.! doctors all over the country are noting aphasia in children with ASD. Basically, nonverbal and minimally-verbal kids often suffer from a form of aphasia similar to that of stroke patients—although their *receptive speech* (comprehension) is fine, they lack *expressive speech* (the ability to talk) for reasons we do not yet understand. When these children become verbal, they usually start speaking in full grammatically-correct sentences, and often explain that they heard and understood everything that was being said around them—and more importantly, *about* them. They just "couldn't get their words out."

Even though it might seem like they're on the planet Zoraq rather than in the same room, never, *ever* forget that there is a child in there absorbing every word they hear.

Speech and comprehension take place in two entirely different parts of the brain, and can operate independently. Which explains a lot of people whose ability to produce words appears to far outstrip their ability to comprehend them… sort of a reverse aphasia. Unfortunately, many of these people work for the CDC.

Family policy

Every family needs to have a firm policy regarding how they will discuss autism within their family. I've made it very clear (even to my husband) that it is flat-out *rude* to discuss someone as though they are not in the room, and it is simply *not allowed* in our family. We also had to decide as a family how much our son should know about his condition. We chose to explain in simple terms how his ASD came about to the best of our understanding, and explain his various treatments in 4-year-old terms. We also let him know that when we share this information with other families it is not to embarrass him, but so that the other parents can keep their kids from getting sick like he did, or to help their child get better.

Think before you speak!

Whenever I have to discuss my son's lack of expressive speech in front of him, I make sure what I am going to say will make him feel good about himself. How would I feel if someone said the same about me? If what you have to say is not positive, it's best kept for a time when you are sure your child isn't within hearing distance.

Cheerleading

It's tough being a cheerleader all the time, but it is truly the most precious gift we can give our kids. On the days when I can't decide whether to laugh or cry, I just give him a big hug, kiss the top of his head, and tell him the truth... that he is the best son any mommy could ever ask for.

The Internet

After a long day, I put my son to bed, tidied up, filled in the daily report, and watched a bit of TV with my husband and dogs. I looked at the clock and decided that if I spent 5–10 minutes and checked my email I could be in bed before 10:30 pm and get a blissfully complete night's sleep.

I sat down at the computer; it took 5 minutes to check the weather for the next few days and delete the trash emails. I skimmed a few messages. A friend had sent me a email regarding some new MB-12 research. I blast a two-line "thank you" note to her and click the attached link. It's very cool research and I get to the bottom and a couple of people are asking questions. Someone asks a question I had been curious about myself. I click on the link and begin my descent. Several people responded eloquently, including one person who routinely posts on every e-list and blog within seconds of new research coming out, discounting all of it completely. (We all know the ones—ever wonder who pays their bills? Anyway, for the story's sake we will refer to him from here on as *narcissus*.) A mother posts about her success with the new recommended dosages, and *narcissus* blasts her, spewing the usual anti-biomedical propaganda. I start opening windows—I just know I've seen some old research that backs up her claims. Who does this guy *narcissus* think he is … does he even have a child with ASD? I am now rehearsing in my head what I am going to write while searching. Other parents start posting en mass. I email several friends the research I just found to contradict *narcissus*. Funny, they all seem to still be up too.

I check my "sent" messages to make sure I attached the right file. My last message was sent at 1:47 am. Great! It's 1:49 am, I'm exhausted, furious at people I've never met, my mind is going a mile a minute, and my husband is sleeping peacefully in the next room so I don't even have anyone to grumble to. What's worse is that virtually the same thing happened two days ago.

Sound familiar? For us moms the internet is both a blessing and a curse. It is a great research and networking tool but it can be a black hole for our precious free time and serenity.

I created the following "Parental Controls" for myself. It wasn't easy to let go of my old habits

Value your time

I took a good hard look at the time I spent online. How did I (or my family) benefit from my time online? How else could I have used my precious free time (hot bath, extra sleep, good book)? I can't get that time back. Was it worth it?

Cut way back

Check your personal email and conduct online "business" twice a week (yes, I said twice a week). I went from going online twice a day to twice a week. I chose Tuesdays and Fridays. The first week was tough—I kept imagining exciting things going on that I was missing... kind of like what our kids think happens when they go to bed. Oddly, when I did check my email there really wasn't anything particularly exciting going on. The sky had not fallen.

Keep an internet "to do" list

I now keep a list on the refrigerator of things I need to do online. If I need to order supplements, research something, or order a book, I put it on the list. Then when I check my email on Tuesday I have an "internet itinerary," so to speak. This kept me from hopping on the computer for a "minute" during the day. It's never a minute. Ever.

Sign off

I signed off of all but two elists, both of which cover ASD news.

Turn off your computer

Literally, *shut it down.* I found I was less likely to pop on the computer after putting towels away if I had to wait for the silly thing to boot up. It saves a lot of phantom electricity, too.

Marriage

The divorce rate among parents of children with ASD is reported by some sources to be well over 70%. As Autism Moms, we could debate the validity of the statistics, or compare the numbers to those of parents with Down Syndrome children, or *we can consider it a friendly warning.* I try to let those stats be a reminder for me to cherish my marriage. To remember that despite the multitude of challenges we face as parents, we have an obligation to each other and our kids to make our marriage the foundation stone for our family. Here are some things that may help as you walk the road of ASD together. (If you are not married, feel free to skip this section.)

Remember your great-grandma

Don't laugh—she was probably married for 70 years. Mine was. I always think of my father's grandmother, beloved by the whole family, to remind myself that passion probably wasn't even among her Top Five reasons for *getting* married. It can be hard for us to feel anything even resembling passion when we are thoroughly burned out. These are the times I remember the other 50 reasons I married my husband (great with kids, cheerful personality, gorgeous, I'd never laughed as hard with anyone before…). Make your own list and pull it out when you are frustrated.

Live in the day

When you do have time together, try not to use it for either projecting ("sifting through the wreckage of the future" as

I like to call it) or trying to figure out what you could have done differently. "Autism guilt" is deadly to a marriage.

Fixers

Remember men are very into fixing things—it's a hallmark of testosterone. And ASD is the ultimate brain teaser... I swear men instinctively view it like a transmission problem in a car. Unfortunately, there appears to be at present no J-B BrainWeld that will fix it—it takes a combination of many things, along with that great enemy of "fixers" everywhere: time. Therefore, autism is an especially huge frustration for men.

Communication and confidences

Women generally have female friends that they can share their fears and joys with. But as wives, often we are the *only* people our husbands confide in, because men rarely confide their fears to other men (testosterone again). Rather than being overwhelmed or annoyed when he tries to share his concerns, I try to see receiving a husband's often ill-expressed confidences as an honor bestowed on a wife.

Monday morning quarterbacking

You might as well just ignore this, because all men do it to some extent. It's really not meant to be hurtful, or to dredge up the past—they are simply just trying to "figure it all out." It's part of that whole "fixing it" thing. A gentle reminder to stay in the present usually helps.

Flirt

I kiss my husband as often as possible, and goose him regularly throughout the day. It's just plain good for morale. Even if it grosses out your kids, it's actually comforting for kids to see their parents as a happy couple.

Remember little ears

All serious conversations about ASD, development (or the lack thereof), marital strife, and strained finances should be adult-only and done in private. And try to schedule them for a time when neither partner is tired, hungry, or cranky. If a conversation on any one of these topics is underway and you realize the timing is bad for any of the above reasons, stop right there and reschedule it.

Don't vent

I vent to my girlfriends when my son has been difficult or I've just had a bad day. Venting to husbands tends to backfire—the information tends to make them feel helpless, which causes them to either go into "fix it" mode, or detach. The results are far more trouble than they're worth when I was simply letting off a little steam. We also may end up shooting ourselves in the foot—if we vent to them *too* often they worry that it's "too much" for us and that we can't handle it. Then they'll *really* make you nuts.

Dinner

Sitters are often not an option for us, so after the kids go to bed, try to have a late, grown-up dinner. Candles, wine glasses, the whole nine yards. Complete with Autism-free conversation. (Think *Dick Van Dyke Show*).

Schedule sex

Seriously, sometimes it seems that everything else takes precedence. Schedule sex for twice a week—you can even put it on your calendar (in code) if you want so you don't forget. We are moms, but we are women first. Sex helps both physiologically and psychologically… research has shown that sexual intercourse causes the release of *vasopressin* in men, and *oxytocin* in women. Both are hormones critical for what evolutionary biologists call "pair-bonding," as well as decreasing levels of the stress hormone *cortisol*. And it's darn good for morale too.

Note: When you think you'd rather just go to sleep, ask your husband for a back rub—he just may be able to change your mind.

Quiet time

After a long, crazy day make a bowl of popcorn and watch a goofy movie with your husband and pets.

Marriage comes first

Making your marriage the focal point of your family takes a great deal of pressure off of your child. Very often the child with ASD feels as though the whole thing is dependent upon him. That is a huge amount of pressure for a little kid.

Credit where credit is due

Not to sound like June Cleaver but… when your husband comes home, try to remember that he worked all day, too, which we tend to forget. Granted, he got to hang out with adults, and probably doesn't have jelly on the front of his shirt, but give him a kiss anyway, let him spend a little time with his happy and healthy kids, and enjoy his company. Who does what or who does *more* is not a game to play if your goal is a stress-free home life.

Don't shout

I know I said it doesn't work on kids, but frankly it doesn't work on husbands either. First and foremost, it's rude and makes us look unhinged. Second, as soon as you raise your voice, most men get defensive and simply stop listening. Third, it will inevitably remind them of their mom, which is rarely a good thing. And finally, it will set our kids spinning (often literally) and that isn't fair to anyone.

It's not easy

ASD is very tough on dads, too. Remember it has, for the present, taken away some dreams they kept very close to their heart. This is the boy who was going to play football at their alma mater, or the little girl they were going to walk down the isle. Right now they are having a hard time envisioning any of those tightly-held dreams ever coming true. Many of our husbands can't let themselves believe that their kids will recover—they don't want to get their hopes up only to have them dashed again. Yet despite all of this, they mix supplements, suffer through gluten-free cookies, go to a litany of therapies, watch movie credits over and over, pay incredible medical bills, spend time with all the kids, and still think we are the most beautiful woman they've ever met.

CHAPTER SIX

Accentuate the Positive

Against the backdrop of World War II, Harold Arlen and Johnny Mercer wrote this tune and it ended up defining a generation. You will find the chorus below. Read it, download it, sing it, dance to it, teach it to your child and most importantly: live it each and every day!

You've got to accentuate the positive
Eliminate the negative
And latch on to the affirmative
Don't mess with Mr. In-between

You've got to spread joy up to the maximum
Bring gloom down to the minimum
Have faith, or pandemonium's liable to walk upon
the scene

Southern wisdom

There's an old expression in the south, "If momma ain't happy, ain't nobody happy." Being happy, even in the craziest of venues, is a *conscious decision*. We can *choose* to be happy today, even if its simply out of defiance to ASD's grip on our lives.

Paint the right picture

I have to admit I was stung when my mother brought this up; it stung, of course, because it was true. She told me I was painting a bleak public portrait of my son, and that because they spend less time with him, family and friends based their opinions of my son solely upon the information I give them. How do my comments describe my son to others? As a stunningly beautiful, bright and funny little boy, or as simply nonverbal and gastrointestinally challenged? The choice is mine. Being thoughtful in what I say about my son sets the foundation for other's opinions of him, and has actually drastically changed other people's attitudes towards him.

Lighten up

ASD is not usually a terminal illness. Our children are not dying. OK, so they can behave strangely and have many challenges to face, but they are essentially happy, getting healthier every day, and learning to enjoy the fascinating world around them. Their lives are not a collective tragedy. Quite the opposite—our little guys are gleefully conquering Autism as we know it. This is definitely cause for celebration!

Find the humor

Finding humor in our kids' behavior can be challenging at first. It's scary to see your child spinning, flapping, rolling on the ground, or sprinkling things in front of his eyes. The problem is that recovery *takes time*. If we want to survive this without turning into grim and unlikable people, we need to acclimate ourselves to the "disturbing" behaviors and find a little humor in them. If your child starts to spin, spin *with* them, or try flapping—it's actually pretty much fun, and it changes isolating behaviors into social behaviors. If the whole family gets going, it invariably starts to look like old film footage of Woodstock.

Early on I decided the word "stimming" was just... well... dumb. (It's always seemed more like self-*soothing* than self-*stimulating* behavior to me, anyway. I have no idea who coined the term, but I suspect it was a shrink.) Around our family, we refer to this weirdness as "being in Captain Jack Sparrow mode" or just "Capt. Jack" for short. (The reasons should be obvious to anyone who's watched *Pirates of the Caribbean*®.) My mom will take one look at him on a particularly weird day and greet him with, "So... how's it goin', Capt. Jack?" And I realized my very serious husband would be just fine when, on a particularly goofy day, he christened my son's pool float "The Black Pearl."

Let others off the hook

Having a sense of humor about our kids' behaviors helps make those around us more comfortable. When my son is behaving strangely in public and others aren't sure how to react, I routinely smile and shrug. "You'll have to excuse us, we're having a "Rain Man" kind of day," I explain. No matter how stressful the scene, this invariably defuses the situation for us, because it's something people with no experience with autism outside of that one movie can easily understand. I have to admit, the first few times I did this I felt the bile rise in the throat, but I found that making others more comfortable around my son was well worth my few seconds of discomfort.

Note: Before you grumble, please go and rent *Rain Man*. Bernard Rimland, Ph.D. prepared Dustin Hoffman for the role himself. It really is a beautiful portrayal of acute autism. Admittedly, for me the movie hit a pretty sensitive nerve; I sure don't like to envision my son doing the same things as an adult that he did when he was a sensory-overloaded three-year-old. But it helps to remember we've

ACCENTUATE THE POSITIVE

come a very long way in treating autism since the 1988 release of *Rain Man.*

Half full

I have one or two other ASD moms with whom I grumble and share stories and concerns about my son's behavior. When anyone else (including my husband) calls and asks how my son is doing, I tell them all the wonderful or funny things he did today. I know perfectly well what his *difficulties* are, I just don't see any point in cataloguing them. I know I'd be far less likely to try new things if *my* every move was critiqued and reported on to everyone who asked. Our kids are doing their very best and should be applauded for their successes, not reminded of what they have yet to accomplish.

Memories last a lifetime

My husband has wonderful memories of sitting on his mom's lap being asked, "How did you get so smart?" or "What is it that makes you so sweet?" These were not rhetorical questions—she wanted *answers.* My husband remembers walking away bursting with pride, searching his mind for exactly how it was that he ended up so terrific. I now ask my son the same questions and hope that when he is an adult he will have the same wonderful memories.

Play

Have fun! Fool around, wrestle, smoosh, splash, spin, roll, bounce and crash. Because he is nonverbal, I was my son's very first playmate. Like many kids with ASD, he needed to be taught how to play. As moms we wear many hats—some days it's multicolored with a little pinwheel on top.

Keep the faith

We all had secret dreams and aspirations for our kids tucked away in our hearts. I know that some days it's hard to believe that our children will be able to achieve all of these dreams, but our kids are intuitive, smart, and very courageous. There is nothing they can't do. Unwavering faith isn't for sissies, but if we don't believe in our children, who will?

A Mother's Gift

This is not the childhood I would have chosen for my son. It is, however, the only one he is going to get. Autism has already stolen so very much from him; I will be *damned* if I will let it snatch a happy childhood from him as well. The day he was born, I promised my baby boy a happy and beautiful childhood and that is exactly what he is going to get.

CHAPTER SEVEN

Pre-screened Resources

Though certainly not complete, the following is a list of "Mom Recommended" resources that you can look to for solid information.

Book List

Autism (informational)

Changing the Course of Autism, **Bryan Jepson, MD**
Covers a huge number of topics for this multisystemic condition. If you don't have a D.A.N.! doctor, but have a good primary care physician, give them a copy of this book so they can better help your child.

Autism Sourcebook, **Karen Ekkorn**
A nice overview of treatments, issues, and various options available. Well-organized and an easy read.

Diets & Cookbooks

The Kid Friendly ADHD and Autism Cookbook,
Pamela Compart and Dana Laake
Great descriptions of the different diets and good recipes.

The Gluten Free Gourmet Bakes Bread, **Bette Hagman**
A must have if your kid loves bread, crackers, pancakes, etc. The recipes may seem complex at first glance, but they are mostly "combine dry, blend wet, and mix together." And they are delicious! Soft with lovely crusts, you'd never

imagine the author's breads were gluten-free. By using ghee instead of butter and almond meal instead of powdered milk, her recipes easily become casein-free. I highly recommend her dessert cookbook as well.

Incredible, Edible Gluten-free Food for Kids,
Sheri Saunderson
Good recipes, a nice troubleshooting section for bakers.

Betty Crocker's Cookbook (pre 1980)
A great way to learn how to cook from scratch. Always has a chapter to cover the basics of cooking. A perfect place to start.

The Joy of Cooking (pre 1980)
Irma S. Rombauer and Marion Rombauer Becker
A great way to learn the basics. Includes explanations of what various ingredients *do* in a recipe.

The Feingold Diet, **Benjamin Fiengold, MD**
The father of the dietary revolution. Established a diet for preventing ADHD and helping food sensitive kids. Clear and concise explanation of the effects of Phenols on our kids.

Feed Your Kids Right, **Lendon Smith**
One of the first (in 1970 this was pretty radical stuff) to recognize spectrum behaviors as multisystemic, and to recommend nutritional and biomedical rather than pharmaceutical treatment to improve behavior.

The Yeast Connection, **William G. Crook**
A nice clear explanation of the effects of overabundance of yeast, celiac disease, and treatment options.

Environmental

Holler For Your Health: Be the Key to a Healthy Family, **Theresa Holler**
A well-organized resource for all your household environmental concerns. Provides a synopsis of available research and simple things you can do in your own home.

Healthy Child, Healthy World, **Christopher Gavigan**
Covers a large number of topics from organic foods to safe insect killers. A great household guide.

Immune System

In Defense of Self, How the Immune System Really Works, **William R. Clark**
Though a very complex subject, Dr. Clark puts the workings of the immune system into layman's terms as well as anyone.

Family and Friends

10 Things Every Autistic Child Wishes You Knew, Ellen Notbohn

Sensitive and thorough, this is a great overview of the challenges of ASD. Perfect for helping others better understand our kids.

All About My Brother, Sara Peralta

Written by an 8-year-old girl, this is a must read for the brothers and sisters of children on the spectrum. A truly beautiful book.

The Autism Acceptance Book, Ellen Sabinis

Compiled as a workbook of sorts, this is a great book for children trying to be friends with a child with ASD.

Potty Training

Toilet Training for Individuals with Autism or Other Developmental Issues, Maria Wheeler, M. ED.

A clear and simple guide with lots of good advice. Great troubleshooting/common mistakes section to help us avoid problems before they happen.

Recovery Stories

Louder Than Words, Jenny McCarthy

Honest and intuitive, this is an empowering story of recovery with particular emphasis on the difficulties we face as moms of ASD kids. **Note:** adult language.

A Real Boy, Christina Adams

Heartfelt and very honest, this book contains a great deal of research information and a beautiful story of recovery.

Son Rise, Barry Neil Kaufman

A wonderful story of one family's struggle and success. A bit dated (the "son" is now a grown man who can be seen speaking at autism conferences worldwide) but a great resource.

Education

How to Raise an Amazing Child the Montessori Way, Tim Seldin

A must read for those trying to create a sensory friendly environment for our kids to learn.

1001 Great Ideas for Teaching and Raising Children with Autism Spectrum Disorders, Ellen Notbohm and Veronica Zysk.

A perfect book for parents, teachers, caretakers, homeschoolers, you name it. A great resource!

What Your Kindergartener Needs to Know,
E.D. Hirsch Jr. and John Holdren
A great guide for preparing your child for school, working on meaningful play or putting together a homeschool plan. **Note:** there is also a book covering all the primary grades.

***The Homeschooling Handbook,* Mary Griffith**
Perfect guide for anyone considering homeschooling, covers history, legal aspects, expenses, and offers great resource lists.

***Negotiating The Special Education Maze: A Guide for Parents and Teachers,* by Deidre Hayden, Cherie Takemoto, Winifred Anderson, and Stephen Chitwood**
Covers the ins and outs of the public school special education system. Very informative and empowering as we push our way through the red tape.

Sensory & Therapy

Note: I used these books to help us make educated decisions regarding our son's therapy protocol. There were several times I wished that I had read all of these *before* we started rather than after.

***The Out of Sinc Child,* Carol Stock Kravowitz**
A clear and concise guide to Sensory Integration Disorders.

The Out of Sinc Child Plays, **Carol Stock Kravowitz**
A guide for purposeful play. A great backup for occupational therapy.

When the Brain Can't Hear, **Teri James Bellis, Ph.D.**
A wonderful and well-written guide to Auditory Processing Disorders and their treatment.

Understanding Applied Behavior Analysis,
Albert J. Kearney
The only book I found that actually describes what ABA is and how it works.

Seeing Through New Eyes, **Melvin Kaplan**
A really interesting look at how vision problems can result in seemingly unrelated physical and behavioral problems and how prism lenses can help resolve them.

Note: For information on the biochemistry behind these visual problems, see marymegson.com.

The Oxygen Revolution,
Paul G. Harch, M.D. and Virginia McCullough
Everything you always wanted to know about Hyperbaric Oxygen Therapy.

Websites

ageofautism.com
An online newsletter, AOA is a great way to keep abreast of new research, medical issues and follow what is happening with regard to autism in Washington.

autism.com
Autism Research Institute. New parent info. D.A.N.! Doctor lists, research, recovery—it's all here!

Autismcoach.com
Good informational site with nice research and supplement sections.

Californiahyperbarics.com
California Intergrative Hyperbaric Center is solid therapy facility with a great staff. A nice resource for those on the west coast.

EPA.gov
Not particularly user friendly but if you ignore the fish propaganda and various levels you can find clear maps of mercury and lead emissions nationwide.

Functionalmedicine.org
The Institute for Functional Medicine. Though not necessarily D.A.N.! Doctors, this is a group of doctors that is usually very comfortable working with the multisystemic issues we face with autism.

Generationrescue.org

Generation Rescue is a great spot for news, recovery stories, and resources. It also has a great alternative vaccine schedule.

ICDRC.org

Home to well-known D.A.N.! doctors Jeff Bradstreet, MD, and Dan Rossignol, MD. Creations Own and the International Child Development Resource Center (ICDRC) websites boast an incredible amount of information for families and cutting edge research. The facility itself is wonderful and the staff is caring and knowledgeable.

Megson.com

Mary Megson, MD, head of The Pediatric and Adolescent Ability Center is one of the best. A wonderful clinician and researcher, Dr. Megson is leading the charge. The website contains some incredible research and information for parents of children with ASD and other developmental issues. The staff is fantastic and truly dedicated to their patients' recovery.

projectlifesaver.org

Project Lifesaver is a nationwide tracking program established to locate and rescue missing persons, namely those with cognitive impairments and developmental disabilities who wander. Contact your local sheriffs department to see if this program is available in your area.

Rimlandcenter.org
Named for Bernard Rimland PhD, autism pioneer and founder of the Autism Research Institute, the Rimland Center for Integrative medicine is a training facility for health care professionals as well as a doctors office specializing in biomedical & therapeutic intervention Elizabeth Mumper, MD, is the center's Director.

Safeminds.org
Provides solid information on the links between mercury and neurological damage, Safeminds sponsors some cutting-edge research.

Talkaboutcuringautism.org
TACA is a wonderful resource for families in all phases of recovery. A perfect place for news, research, medical resources and networking. TACA has an incredible mentoring program for parents interested in learning more about treating autism.

thoughtfulhouse.org
Located in Austin, TX, and founded by gastroenterologist Andrew Wakefield, Thoughtful House is a clinic specializing in integrative approach to treating kids with an array of problems. Lots of good information on this site.

vitacost.com
Vitacost has a huge selection of supplements, natural personal care & cleaning supplies. You can expect super low prices, inexpensive one-price shipping & fast service.

wisconsinhyperbaric.com

Wisconsin Integrative Hyperbaric Center is an incredible facility that offers biomedical and therapy based treatment. Kyle Van Dyke, MD, Dan Rossingnol, MD, Kenneth Stoller, MD, and the entire WIHC staff are dedicated to treating the whole child and helping families through every phase of recovery.

Family Restaurants

Some national chain restaurants are pretty autism-friendly, and some are decidedly less so. (Some are downright awful.) So everyone doesn't have to reinvent the Restaurant Wheel when they are on the road, here's a list of some of the most ASD Friendly.

And the winner is…

Bob Evans®
(Didn't see *that* one coming, did you?)

Bob Evans restaurant is a fairly quiet and visually calm family restaurant. Late mornings (stay away on weekends) or early evenings are probably the best times to visit. The staff tends to be very accommodating and willing to go the extra mile if you give them a heads-up. Bob Evans possesses the best kid menu, bar none. With a dozen sides to choose from, this is a great place for GFCF kids. All the vegetables except the carrots can be cooked without butter, and the ingredients and allergen information for the entire menu is available online. Though Bob Evans is predominantly located in the midwest and on the east coast, they have acquired the Mimi's Café Restaurants on the west coast and will be incorporating most of their menu items into Mimi's existing menu.

Ruby Tuesday®
Tends to be quiet midweek and the atmosphere is not too visually stimulating. Though it has a limited kids menu, the staff is very resourceful and the kitchen staff is flexible.

Applebee's®

Can be visually stimulating for some kids, but they are flexible with their kids' menu, and pretty accommodating.

The Olive Garden®

Nice quiet environment, flexible staff, good kids' menu. Not a good choice if your kid is GFCF, though—Italy's cuisine pretty much revolves around gluten.

Shoney's® Restaurant

A good option for "starving" kids. Offering buffet style dining, Shoney's has choices enough to accommodate virtually any diet. The low-key décor and helpful staff make it good choice if you need food fast.

Honorable mention:

Chick-Fil-A®

Though more "fast food" than "family restaurant," it is a great option if diet allows. Their food contains very few allergens and Chick-Fil-A is a great supporter of Autism research and the Autism Community as a whole.

Cracker Barrel®

Good menu and fantastic staff—however, negotiating your way through the cluttered "Country Store" can trigger sensory overload in our kids.

T-shirts, pins, etc.

Many of the website listed in the previous section sell t-shirts and other accessories but if you haven't found what you are looking for try the following site:

Cafepress.com

Has thousands of Autism-related items for sale. If you don't see what you are looking for, you can have it made, and your design will join the "autism list" and can then be purchased by other moms.

Disney World® is a registered trademark of Disney Enterprises, Inc., Burbank, CA; Ener-G Egg Replacer® is a registered trademark of Ener-G Foods, Inc., Seattle, WA; Coca-Cola Classic® is a registered trademark of Coca-Cola Company, Atlanta, GA; Busch Gardens® is a registered trademark of Anheuser-Busch, Incorporated, St. Louis, MO; SeaWorld® is a registered trademark of Sea World, Inc., St. Louis MO; Yummy Earth Lollipops® is a registered trademark of YummyEarth LLC LTD, Ridgewood NJ; Trader Joe's lollipops® is a registered trademark of Trader Joe's Company, Monrovia CA; SwyFlotter® is a registered trademark of Kiss My Face Corporation, Gardiner, NY; Netflix® is a registered trademark of Netflix, Inc., Los Gatos, CA; Seventh Generation® is a registered trademark of Seventh Generation, Inc., Burlington, VT; Bob Evans® is a registered trademark of Bob Evans Restaurants of Michigan, Inc., Ann Arbor, MI; Ruby Tuesday® is a registered trademark of RTBD, Inc., Maryville, TN; Applebee's Grill® is a registered trademark of Applebee's International, Inc., Overland Park, KS; The Olive Garden Café® is a registered trademark of General Mills Restaurants, Inc., Orlando, FL; Shoney's Restaurant® is a registered trademark of Shoney's, Inc., Nashville, TN; Cracker Barrel® is a registered trademark of Cracker Barrel Old Country Store, Inc., Lebanon, TN; *Pirates of the Caribbean®* is a registered trademark of Disney Enterprises, Inc., Burbank CA; Rice Chex® is a registered trademark of Chex, Inc. Minneapolis, MN; Lea & Perrins® is a registered trademark of ProMark Brands Inc., Meridian ID; FryDaddy® is a registered trademark of National Presto Industries, Inc. Eau Claire, WI; Mr. Potato Head® is a registered trademark of Hasbro, Inc. Pawtucket, RI; Little People® is a registered trademark of Mattel, Inc., El Segundo, CA; Ritalin® is a registered trademark of Novartis AG., Basel Switzerland; Amtrak® is a registered trademark of National Railroad Passenger Corporation (AMTRAK), Washington D.C.; Jell-o® is a registered trademark of Kraft Foods Holdings, Inc., Northfield, IL; Mountain Dew® is a registered trademark of PEPSICO, Inc., Purchase, NY

Notes